WHAT TEACHERS ACROSS
ARE SAYING ABOUT *YOGA AND JUDAISM*:

"I was happy to read your book titled 'Yoga and Judaism'. It is an innovated joy and thought provoking gift, not only for Yogis and Jews, but for all peoples regardless of race, creed, color and personal beliefs. I congratulate you, Steven, for writing this book which is written in such a beautiful and simple way with so much wisdom...I feel like using the same mantra that God used when He first met Adam and Eve. He said according to the Bible, 'Tov M'od...Very Good!'."

Rabbi Joseph H. Gelberman, PhD
President, All Faiths Seminary International
President, Rabbinical Seminary International
President, The New Synagogue
Founder, Interfaith College International
Author, *Physician of the Soul, Zen Judaism,* and
other titles

"Out of the wilderness of confusion and the separation among belief systems is brought forth a clarity of understanding which brings to light a synthesis appropriate for today's thinking. Steve Gold, from extensive study and experience, presents a fresh perspective which leads back to the root of major religions. Interspersed with humor, provocative seriousness and practical application, this book is a must for those desiring to see the spirituality, as well as the commonality of our belief systems, in a new light of time. The reader will find a greater enhancement of his or her understanding as Steve Gold unifies through understanding that which the structures have separated."

Shirley Chambers
Founder/Director, Karin Kabalah Center, Atlanta, GA
Author, *Kabalistic Healing* and *Kabalah: A Process of Awakening*

"This wonderful gift of understanding of the unity of all approaches to spiritual unfoldment grew from the seeds of love and wisdom planted in Steve's mind and heart through the compassionate teachings of Sri Swami Rama of the Himalayas, complemented by Steve's own systematic and faithful endeavors to practice and actualize in his daily life and silent study and contemplations authentic Vedantic and yogic disciplines. Steve's life and interior researches have happily made available to a wider public these ancient, yet vitally relevant approaches to the truth for the betterment of all humanity. Much appreciation to you, Steve, for your life and works!"

Maa Sewa Bharati
Rishikesh, the Himalayas

OM SHALOM:

YOGA

AND

JUDAISM

EXPLORATIONS OF A JEWISH YOGI

SECOND EDITION

Steven J. Gold, זרח

ACKNOWLEDGEMENTS

The author gratefully acknowledges assistance, encouragement and inspiration provided by Rabbi Joseph H. Gelberman, Shirley Chambers, Maa Sewa Bharati, my wife Elaine, and my two sons, Tomas and Daniel.

Thanks to Eric Sprung for selflessly assisting with the graphics, and Kirk Ivey at Printlogic for additional technical assistance.

Special thanks and blame go to Elayne Herris Baskin. This is all your fault! If you hadn't sent me "The Kabbalah Deck" for my birthday a few years ago, none of this would have happened.

PERMISSIONS

Excerpts from the following works have been reprinted with permission:

Living with the Himalayan Masters, by Swami Rama, Himalayan Institute Press, Honesdale, PA.

Zohar, the Book of Splendor, by Gershom Scholem, copyright 1949 and renewed 1977 by Schocken Books, a division of Random House, Inc.

God is a Verb, Kabbalah and the Practice of Mystical Judaism, by Rabbi David A. Cooper, Riverhead Books, The Berkley Publishing Group, a division of Penguin Group (USA) Inc.

Sefer Yetzirah, by Aryeh Kaplan, Red Wheel/Weiser, Newburyport, MA and San Francisco, CA.

About the cover: Detail of a thangka (Tibetan canvas painting framed by material) designed by the author adapting a traditional Tibetan image, produced by Happy Valley Store, Bhaktipur, Nepal. Placed in the center of the six-pointed star symbolizing the Heart center in the Yoga tradition, the Mogen David/Star(Shield) of David/Jewish Star in the Jewish tradition, is the Sanskrit letter symbolizing the mother of all mantras, the origin of all sound, "Om", which emanates out of The Silence beyond.

This book is dedicated to the memories of Dr. Leon J. Yagod, Rabbi, and Swami Rama of the Himalayas. I am so happy that Rabbi Yagod lived long enough to see me begin the process that culminated in the writing of this book; and to behold that the training he provided me for my Bar Mitzvah enabled me to train my two sons for theirs. Concerning Swami Rama, only others who knew him can appreciate how special it is that he regarded me as one of his spiritual sons. I am forever grateful for having been accepted under the protective, guiding and nurturing wings of such a wondrous spiritual tradition.

CONTENTS

Preface to Second Edition

There were two main reasons that spurred creation of this second edition. First was a need to correct a few matters that have been brought to my attention, and second was a desire to expand the chapter on Jewish Yoga Meditation and add a new chapter on Jewish Healing Meditation.

For one correction, I reworked a portion in Chapter Five discussing the confusion over Ein/Ayin whereby I myself had become confused and thus added to the confusion. I misstated that all the words that phonetically sound like "ein" or "ayin" are spelled with the letter "aleph", whereas some are actually spelled with the letter "ayin". My gratitude to Rabbi Yaacov Kravitz for bringing this to my attention. I also added to this mix a new discussion concerning the word designating a well/spring. With the newly-worked clarification, I hope to have better articulated the various issues concerning the confusion, without adding to it.

The other correction is also in Chapter Five in the discussion about kundalini shakti, another subject matter over which there has been much confusion. After receiving clarification from sources within my own yoga tradition which were further substantiated in great detail by another wonderful source discussed below, I have corrected the statement in the first edition that "kundalini shakti is a particular manifestation of concentrated pranic energy", replacing it with the following: "although there has been some confusion about referring to kundalini shakti as a type of concentrated pranic energy, there is an alternative and more accurate view that it is a mysterious power of consciousness more subtle than and distinguished from energy". The other source referred to above is the book, *Kundalini Vidya, The Science of Spiritual Transformation, A Comprehensive System for Understanding and Guiding Spiritual Development,* by Joan Shivarpita Harrigan, Ph.D. This is the most comprehensive, detailed and well-researched book on the subject matter I have to date encountered. Dr. Harrigan, aided by the guidance of Swami Chandrasekharanand Saraswati, has created an excellent source book that, despite its extensive research, is not couched in the abstruse language of a scholarly tome, but is rather quite easily accessible and readable. It deftly combines inspirational passages with detailed information obviously based upon direct experience and not just intellectual knowledge. It provided answers and clarity to many little questions and fuzzy details that have nagged at me over the years. I commend this book to anyone who has an interest in the subject matter as contained in the title and subtitles.

Concerning the additional material on meditation, since the publishing of the first edition, the analytics from my author's blog indicates a great interest in Jewish meditation and Hebrew mantras. I therefore added a section to Chapter Eight, summarizing blog entries I have made which further explain the interface of yoga-based mantra meditation techniques utilizing Biblical Hebrew phrases in place of Sanskrit phrases. Both are considered revealed sacred languages, and I believe such phrases in either language, properly employed in suitable meditation techniques, carry profound spiritual benefits.

There has been increasing focus over the years in various avenues for healing in addition to Western medicine, including healing meditation practices. This is an area for which I, somewhat shamefully, never had much interest. My general perspective had been that meditation in and of itself is a significant tool for self-healing. Individuals healed through their own meditation practices would then create a spill-over effect into their environment and in their interchanges with their fellow beings. However, out of curiosity, I attended an introductory presentation on "Pranic Healing" as formulated by the late Master Choa Kuk Sui, and decided to take the initial training. Attending this course impressed upon me the importance of more directly aiding the healing of others, and challenged me to ponder what kind of approach would feel most comfortable for me. As a result of these musings, a formulation for a Jewish Healing Meditation came to me that I first published on my blog, and which I am now incorporating as a new Chapter Nine in this Second Edition (whereby the former Chapter Nine has now become Chapter Ten). It is a synthesis of three main sources: it borrows and builds upon some of the principles I learned in the Pranic Healing Course, in conjunction with some tweaks to basic breathing, relaxation and stress management techniques I learned through my study of yoga, and further incorporates principles from the mystical Jewish tradition. In keeping with my own personal introverted pre-disposition towards internalized methods, intentional procedures and interventions, as such, are kept to a minimum and are all enacted silently within. While this may sound like a New Age mish-mash, I feel it is a very profound and effective technique founded in time-tested traditions, updated for our current circumstances whereby many elements of world spiritual healing cultures are melding, resulting in the emergence of new forms. I invite the reader to try it for themselves, approaching it with an open heart and mind, and come to their own conclusions.

Lastly, as long as I was undertaking a new edition, I felt I might as well try my hand at enhancing the aesthetic presentation with some different fonts and formatting of the text, distinguishing it a bit more from the bare-bones basics of the first edition. Also, as a final effort to polish up and improve the overall quality of the book, I enlisted the assistance of some volunteer editors. Together, we combed through the text of the first edition and the content additions and revisions I made for the second edition, resulting in many stylistic editing revisions. I hope the reader finds this new edition to their liking.

My heartfelt gratitude goes out to the afore-mentioned selfless servants who provided wonderful editorial assistance that has greatly enhanced the clarity and quality of the finished product: my wonderful wife Elaine, Steven Weiniger, Katherine Robinsun and Marty Rosenman.

Introduction

Om Shalom...

Yoga and Judaism. Two vast subjects, each of which encompasses thousands of pages of primary texts and scriptures, as well as thousands of pages more in commentary and supplemental materials, ancient, modern, and on-going. So what am I doing adding another drop into this vast ocean? Believe me, it wasn't something I undertook lightly or voluntarily. All I can say is that it was something I was given to do. So here it is.

I confess. I'm Jewish, and I'm a yogi. I'm a Jewish yogi. As a child, I studied Judaism. As a young adult, I studied yoga. As an older adult, I studied Judaism again, in the light of yoga. I started seeing connections, a lot of fascinating connections from which the seed of this book originated and grew. But before I get ahead of myself, let me start with the beginning seed, which was my adult study of Torah...

Torah is and has been many things to many people. On the physical level, a Torah is a parchment scroll on which is hand-written in the ancient language of Biblical Hebrew that portion of the Old Testament known as the Five Books of Moses: Genesis, Exodus, Leviticus, Numbers and Deuteronomy. As with the Sanskrit Vedas from the Eastern Tradition, which many maintain are emanations which emerged from a Divine Source through the ancient meditative Rishis, to some, these words on the Torah Scroll are all Divine Revelation and Sacred Scripture that have been faithfully and accurately recorded without revision or deviation from the time first revealed to Moses up to the present time. To others within the Jewish tradition, it is something less than that, but still something of great value and significance.

On a multitude of other levels, Torah is more than what is contained in the physical written scroll, which can be seen as a significant, yet fragmentary representation of something much more vast, like the tip of an iceberg. To begin with, there is broad, although not universal, acceptance that accompanying the original written text contained in the scroll was a body of Oral Tradition (the Mishnah, which was eventually rendered into written form), without which the words contained in the written tradition could never be properly understood. And then there is further written elaboration which makes up the Talmud, and yet further elaboration called Midrash. Also, there are the other portions of the Old Testament besides the Five Books of Moses that contribute to the Jewish tradition. And on and on through the ages there have been commentaries and writings of Jewish thinkers up to the present time. Thus has Jewish scripture and thought been recorded and expanded upon, all of which, in a broad sense, can be considered Torah.

Then there are the unspoken and unrecorded levels lying yet further beneath the surface, from which has emanated such wonders as Kabala and Gematria. Reb Zalman Schacter-Shalomi, in his book, *Paradigm Shift*, provides a wonderful illustration of the multi-layered meanings of the words and sentences in the Torah. He takes one phrase from the important Amidah collection of prayers and lays out in graphic format eight different layers of meaning, word by word. Elsewhere, he suggests that there is meaning contained not only in the form of the black written letters, but also in the white forms the letters create on the parchment on which they are written. Torah in its broadest sense is a fathomless, multilayered, breathing microcosm/macrocosm and blueprint of life itself. Perhaps not only a blueprint, a representation; perhaps it is Life Itself.

* * *

So how did this book, this sliver off of the iceberg, come to be? Well, that's a long story, but I'll try to make it short. I'm a baby-boomer who grew up in suburban New Jersey, born to a Jewish family. Although we were not very observant from a religious practice point of view, there was still a certain ethnic/cultural Jewish upbringing. I did go to Hebrew school at a Modern Orthodox synagogue, not because of my family's beliefs, but because it happened to be conveniently located a couple of blocks away from where we lived. The saga of my particular life was not uncommon for a person of my generation. I always had a certain religious/spiritual bent, but when I reached late adolescence I went through an atheist period, rejecting the juvenile conception of God that had been inculcated from my Hebrew school days. During my college years and beyond, this led to a fairly typical search for a refined spiritual meaning. I became exposed to eastern spirituality, and eventually settled into serious spiritual growth through a lineage known as The Tradition of the Himalayan Masters, propagated in the West by the late Swami Rama of the Himalayas and through the organization he founded, The Himalayan Institute of Yoga Science and Philosophy.

Throughout my development into adulthood, although I was happy with my spiritual progress through my association with this ancient yogic tradition, grounded in a traditional meditation practice, I also wondered about my Jewish background and if and how I should be relating to my Jewish roots. I would experiment at times through various avenues to try to approach Judaism, but often met with dead-ends. I continued to receive subtle messages from my spiritual mentor, Swami Rama, that I should somehow explore Judaism. As my particular spiritual bent was grounded in meditation and mysticism, with no interest in ritual observance which is prevalent in most Jewish practice, I tried once again to attempt to approach Judaism through its mystical side, Kabala. I hooked up with the Karin Kabalah Center in Atlanta, where I had settled in my adult life, only to find it was based on Christian Kabala, although it still had its foundation in Jewish Kabala. I nevertheless found the substance and practices of this course fascinating, and I engaged in this extensive and deep course of study which lasted two and a half years. One emphasis in this particular course was that although it had an intellectual component, it was not primarily an intellectual exercise. Rather, it was basically an inner experiential transformative process, addressing the unconscious through guided meditations utilizing powerful archetypal symbols in accord with the ideas of Carl Jung and Joseph Campbell.

At the conclusion of this course of study, partly due to a suggestion by the principle teacher and architect of the course, Shirley Chambers, and partly through being otherwise led, I began a self-directed course of study of Jewish sources, and finally found doors opening through which I felt comfortable and connected. During the early stages of this process, it became evident to me that it would be most helpful to first approach the source upon which all of these other teachings were based, the primary text of the written Torah itself. So my other readings continued but became secondary to a primary endeavor of studying the Torah, timed in coordination with the weekly portion traditionally read in temples and synagogues around the world.

I first read and studied the text and commentaries, along with the related Haftorah, from two currently popular translations, *The Chumash*, Stone Edition of the Artscroll Series, Rabbis Nosson Scherman and Meir Zlotowitz, General Editors, and *The Living Torah*, by Rabbi Aryeh Kaplan. Early in this process, I decided it would be a good idea to write summaries of the weekly portions, focusing mostly on a succinct summary of the text itself, but also recording observations and highlights of various matters that particularly caught my attention in the texts and the commentaries. Writing those summaries initiated a further process that eventually culminated in writing this book. I have since learned that such summarizing and commenting on Torah portions is a traditional practice among Torah students, know as D'var Torah. The summaries themselves may at some time be published as a companion volume. However, this book eventually evolved out of a series of talks/workshops I conducted at the Karin Kabbalah Center, further expressing insights, connections and syntheses between the three major traditions in which I have practiced and studied: Traditional Judaism, including Jewish Kabala and mysticism; what I loosely call the Western Mystical Tradition, particularly as embodied in the teachings at the Karin Kabbalah Center, but which includes other branches such as traditional Theosophy and other Western Esoteric schools; and the traditional Indian system of Yoga and Vedanta, especially as taught through the Himalayan Institute.

What I found most interesting about this entire process was that, like the Kabala course, the very act of sitting down and engaging in this study became obviously much more than a mere intellectual process. I could discern that it was an experiential process of inner spiritual growth and transformation on a deep, subtle, unconscious level, and thus its magic and its power. My earnest hope is that the reader of this little tome will find inspiration, stimulation, maybe some revelation, and hopefully, most precious of all, perhaps some transformation.

Om Shalom...

Prologue

A great teaching has come forth through Judaism and its Torah. It states that at the commencement of this current creation cycle, issuing forth out of Paradise was a river that flowed to the East to the land of India, a land communicating the highest spiritual truths and wisdom, containing materials that could aid a person to realize the highest of spiritual states.

This "Tara" of India was communicated to Abraham, the first Jew, who declared and disseminated its primary teaching that *All Is One* to lands and people who had long ago forgotten this most basic Truth. He traveled to Egypt, bringing the seed of this Truth to this narrow land. Some of his descendants stayed in the land of Palestine, a major crossroads of the world and a juncture between East and West, to prepare to receive a people who would act as a conduit for this message. Others were sent to India to commune with this land engendering spiritual Truth and prepare to transmit it to their brethren in Palestine for retransmission to the West. Another group of his descendants followed his footsteps into Egypt to gestate the new people who would serve as a conduit for this message of truth.

Moses assisted in birthing this new people, who emerged from the Nile Valley birth canal of its Mother Africa to reside in its cradle and new land. This people was provided the Tara/Torah, which communicated to them the basic spiritual Truth of the Oneness, their mission to live and propagate this teaching, and procedures to carry out their mission of receiving the ongoing pure transmission from their brethren in India.

In accordance with their instructions, a Great Temple was built in Palestine to serve as a prism to facilitate transmission between East and West and sustain the purity of the servants of this transmission.

What happened?

Chapter One

The Center of The World
The Role of Judaism in the World Symphony
Connections Between Three Major Traditions: Judaism, Eastern Mysticism, Western Mysticism

The Center of The World

There is a story from the Jewish tradition about a Roman commander and one of his Jewish captives, a scholarly rabbi, on the way back to Rome after the destruction of the Second Temple in 70 CE. Now, certain persecutors inflict on their victims more than just physical torture and ordeals like throwing them to the lions. For the sake of amusement, some include psychological and intellectual torment, mockery and humiliation. They want to demonstrate not only their physical, military superiority, but also their intellectual and spiritual superiority over their captives. This story involves an exchange between the Roman commander and the Jewish sage, intended by the Roman to highlight the superiority of Rome while tormenting his prisoner. The question from the Roman commander was designed to be a lose-lose situation for his poor Jewish captive: "Where is the center of the world?" The sage immediately recognized this as an intended no-win situation, because from the Roman's point of view, the center of the world was Rome. They had just destroyed the Second Temple and reduced Jerusalem to rubble. The commander knew that if the sage was true to the traditional Jewish belief that Jerusalem was the center of the world, he would have reason to torment his captive more for being so audacious and arrogant, particularly in light of the fact that the Romans had just destroyed Jerusalem. If the sage answered that Rome is the center of the world, the commander would know that the sage was not being true to himself; he was just trying to curry favor, and in doing so, he would be blaspheming his tradition. So the sage was caught in a quandary cleverly concocted by the Roman, as it would appear there were only these two answers. Either way, it would be a lose-lose situation for the sage and a win-win situation for the commander. However, the sage quickly came up with a third answer. At the time, they were somewhere on the way from Jerusalem to Rome, but nowhere of any particular note. He pointed to a place off in the distance that

19

they both could see, and said, "see that spot over there?" "Yes". "That's the center of the world".

The sage gets out of his dilemma with this enigmatic answer, and, as is often the case in Jewish commentary and analysis, his response becomes the subject of thorough scrutiny and interpretation. The basic analysis of the answer is that the sage had come up with more than a clever little escape to extricate himself from his dilemma; he was explicating a profound truth. From a certain point of view, the world is a sphere floating in space. We all know that it turns and has an axis and gravitation and latitudes and longitudes and all that, but from one point of view, the globe is a sphere suspended in space. Regarding the surface of a sphere, where is its center? It can be anywhere; any point on the surface of the sphere can be the center. The sage was propounding that from one point of view, anywhere is the center of the world. He squirmed out of his quandary with his answer, while at the same time providing a deep existential insight.

Examining human history, civilizations, religions, ethnic groups, fraternities, clubs, whatever distinct defined social order it may be, everyone who identifies with any kind of group usually thinks there's something special about their membership in that group. Of course, religion is a big group in which that occurs. If you examine religious and spiritual myths, as delineated by the likes of Joseph Campbell and Carl Jung, most religious groups – whether cannibals in New Guinea, Eskimos near the North Pole, Native Americans, Chinese – most groups are going to have a myth that recites that their tradition goes back to the beginning of time, they are the keepers of a special truth and they reside at the real center of the world. They have a secret, sacred duty and task to carry out that nobody else in the world can do, and if they don't do it, it's not going to get done. They are the guardians of creation. You find that everywhere. A Hopi Indian myth refers to them as the real guardians of the Truth, with a special function that only they could serve. The Chinese referred to their domain as "the middle kingdom', "middle" meaning "central", we're the central focus of creation.

Everyone has that myth. How can they all be true? Much of the conflict in the world involves clashes between personal, ethnic and national egos invested in competing provincial myths. The point of the above story is that in some way, they all can be true. From one perspective, every point is equally a center of the world.

One meaningful metaphor from this perspective is that the world is like a patch-work quilt. Another is that the world is like a symphony. To put it more accurately, life is like a multi-media presentation. There are orchestras, music of every kind conceivable, dancing, performing arts, construction, graphic arts; everything imaginable in this vast multi-media presentation which we know as life on earth. And everyone wants to feel special, to feel pride in themselves and their heritages and traditions, in the roles they are playing in this grand performance. There are two ways to express pride of membership in any given group. One is a positive assertion of the virtues, functions and accomplishments of the group. The other is a negative approach of comparing a group to other groups and distinguishing a particular group as somehow being better than other groups. One group elevates itself by criticizing another, placing itself in a contrasting and better light. Sometimes, the distinctions are taken a step further, often due to a sense of insecurity, of feeling threatened, more often than not a *perceived,* rather than a *real,* threat. Then one group asserts that they have the only truth, and they won't feel safe and secure until contrary groups are eliminated. It goes on and on. It is constantly an issue in political campaigns. There is always an issue concerning when a campaign will go negative. A candidate proclaims, "I'm going to be positive. I'm going to retain a positive approach. I'm just going to promote my image of myself as a good candidate. I'm not going to start criticizing other people." But the question of going negative almost always rears its head. And it is often taken one step further than mere criticism of an opponent. The strategy often becomes that if you want to assure victory, you not only *criticize* your opponent, but in addition, it is best to find a way to *destroy, disable* your opponent. That's been the common practice in politics, and it would appear to bear some insight into the history of world conflict.

Conquest and imperialism often include one group attempting to impose their ways on others, as if theirs is the only valid or superior way. It can be political, nationalistic, ethnic, religious, or some combination. Among religions, certain strains of Christianity and Islam have been particularly intolerant, aggressive and imperialistic. Most other religions acknowledge that there are other valid religions. It is particularly Christianity and Islam that maintain that they are the only one true religion. Everyone else has to convert to us or else! Most Eastern religions are tolerant and accepting to some degree. They may still maintain that theirs is the best way, but they acknowledge that there are other ways. Abraham, considered to be the first Jew, was an active proselytizer. But later on, a practice discouraging conversion developed in Judaism that exists to the current time. Traditional Judaism does not seek converts, and in fact, it is the obligation of traditional Jews to actively discourage conversion, so as not to dissipate purity, to assure sincerity, to maintain exclusivity, whatever the various reasons.

The point is that it would be a really dull world if everyone played violin. Everyone wants to say that they're the crucial element. Some will accept that there are other elements, but they're the most crucial. Without us, everything would fall apart; we're primary, we're essential. Maybe there are others that play a necessary role, but only as "second fiddle". Where does "second fiddle" come from? In the hierarchy of an orchestra, "the Concertmaster", the first chair, first seat violin is the envied position. If you sit next to that person, just one position removed, you're the second fiddle. But the composer composed the piece for all of the parts of the orchestra. One thing that Judaism teaches is that if one single word, one single syllable, one single letter is missing in Torah, the entire world will fall apart. Every single thing that is there is essential. The glockenspiel is just as essential as the Concertmaster. If a particular work designates that the glockenspiel plays three notes in a two hour symphony, those three notes are essential to that two hour symphony, and without it, it's not as the composer intended, it's incomplete, it's imperfect. Now it's hard for any given group to say, "I'm just a glockenspiel." The people who are playing the role of the glockenspiel are very proud that they're the glockenspiel. Maybe they don't envy the first chair, first seat violin, as long as they are given their due respect.

Everything that is here is essential. If every group could have pride in what they are doing, in the function they are performing, in the capacity in which they have been provided to do it, as well as honor each other, we'd be rising to a higher level of human advancement. Instead, there is always this ego identification. The movie, "My Big Fat Greek Wedding," contains a good portrayal of this theme of group pride. It is relatively innocent and comical because the Greeks today aren't a major economic or political power, and aren't involved in any major conflicts. If it was set in Northern Ireland or the Mideast, it would be a different story. But here's the dad, who has this great pride in being Greek, and everything else is secondary to being Greek, everything else is inferior to being Greek. Every word in the universe has its root in Greek. It's cute and comical in that context because it's not threatening. But it makes the point about a pervasive attitude of ethnic superiority. Another movie, "Whale Rider," has the same kind of theme. Here's this little native group in New Zealand that has its own particular myth of creation from time immemorial. They have great pride in their tribal awareness and identity. But they're just this little group in New Zealand. However, they are there doing what they are supposed to be doing. We all have our role and our function.

The Role of Judaism in the World Symphony

The modern Judaism in which I was raised included a sense of persecution. After all, I am only one generation removed from the Holocaust. It still weighs on my parents' generation and on my generation. There is a constant reminder, "we'll never forget, this will never happen again, never again." No one would ever come out and say this about the recent Holocaust because it is too current and it is too painful, but in reading traditional Jewish sources, there is a sense from Jews themselves, that they brought past historic persecutions upon themselves. The Assyrians and Babylonians were agents of God who were punishing them because they didn't live up to their own standards. The Romans, likewise, were agents of God who punished them, and they had it coming. Now, it would be hard for Jews today to say that about the Holocaust, but I have even come across some sense of that very delicately expressed. The more common conception is, "we're victims, we're never going to let this happen again," but there is an underlying sense of "why did this happen to us, why did we have this coming...well maybe we had our own shortcomings, and that's why we had it coming." I was surprised to encounter the expression of that other sentiment.

There are many explanations as to why Jews have been persecuted since time immemorial. One explanation could be that there has been this boastful pride that has been expressed about being more special than anybody else. We're the Chosen People, and nobody else is. We're this exclusive club. We're supposed to be the spiritual leaders of the universe, a "light unto the nations". Well, that kind of attitude breeds resentment, which would appear to be one possible basis for persecution.

In my studies, I've been attempting to identify what is special and unique about Judaism. I have found that many Jewish mystical practices and teachings are similar to those found in Yoga and Theosophy. The Jewish teachers will acknowledge the similarities but then conclude that theirs is better. Even modern teachers who are currently trying to reach out and attract bigger audiences by teaching Kabala and Jewish mysticism will say, for example, yes, there is reincarnation in Judaism, and yes, it does sound a lot like the reincarnation they teach in Yoga, but it's a little different and ours is really better, more accurate and truthful. Yes, there is Jewish meditation, and yes, it does sound a lot like Yoga meditation, but it's different, it's better. Even among many of these more "enlightened", liberalized Jewish teachers, there is still this message that Judaism is the best.

Despite the above criticism concerning bloated ethnic pride and intolerant claims of religious superiority, we should nevertheless look at the world as we know it, and explore what is undeniable about some claims concerning the role of Judaism in our world symphony. If we look at world geography, we know that the British somehow got the monopoly on Zero longitude, running through Greenwich, England, which everyone accepts. It would follow from this designation, as it does in navigation lingo, that everything to the west of Zero longitude would be called "the West" and everything to the east of it would be called "the East". However, navigational designations notwithstanding, even though most of Europe is east of Greenwich, we don't in our common conception regard Europe as being in the

East. What the whole world commonly considers the dividing line, virtually the dividing *point* between East and West, is found at the eastern shore of the Mediterranean, precisely at the location of ancient and modern Israel. Anything west of that is the West, and anything east of that is the East.

Examining world history, we all know that the general area of the Middle East is the birthplace of several major religions: Zoroastrianism, Judaism, Christianity, Islam, the B'Hai Faith. So many Western religions have appeared or originated there, although they have also spread to the East. This area, or nearby Africa, is generally considered to be the Cradle of Civilization.

So there is this reality that the related religions of Judaism, Christianity, and Islam, three of the world's major religions, all originated there. Speaking in terms of Joseph Campbell, one of the basic myths in Judaism is that the Creator, God, the Divine, told those who became the Jewish people that they were supposed to plant themselves right there, right at the juncture between East and West. That is where they're supposed to be, that is their true homeland. It is where all of their revelations occur, and where they're supposed to build a Temple in Jerusalem to serve not only themselves, but all of humankind. Consider how many historical and religious events have occurred in Jerusalem and the surrounding areas.

There are specific instructions in the Torah about how to build this Temple, and one is that the main door is supposed to face East. It is the original "House of the Rising Sun". One conception concerning the functioning of this Temple is that it is to receive and transmit vertical Divine guidance from above; another conception is that it is to receive and transmit lateral Divine guidance from the East. Examining the latitudes between 20 degrees and 45 degrees North, Israel is right in the middle. If you follow the swath between these latitudes eastwardly, you encounter Iraq, Iran, Afghanistan, Pakistan, the entire Himalayan range, North India, Nepal, Tibet, the bulk of mainland China, a good deal of Japan, and crossing over the Pacific, most of the United States. A great deal of the population of the world and the events of world history has existed and taken place within these latitudes. And there are the Hebrew people, in the middle of these latitudes and at the juncture between East and West, planting themselves right there, facing East. This is what we find in exploring this claimed special role of Judaism as the Chosen People in relation to these geographical and historical facts. For whatever reason, they were told to plant themselves at that particular spot, build a Temple there, and face it East. They are to receive and transmit this Divine knowledge and energy, vertically and horizontally. That's what they're supposed to be doing.

Back in the 70's, part of the New Age religious message included a message about "The Dharma [the Way, the Path, the Truth] moving to the West". Many Americans were getting interested in Eastern philosophies and religion: Tibetan

Buddhism, Yoga, Hinduism, Vedanta, Zen, Meditation. "The Dharma", "The Truth", "The Path", the Eastern wisdom that had been lost or had become too crystallized in the West, was getting enlivened again in the East and was moving West. Perhaps it would be more accurate to say it was being *transmitted to* the West rather than it was *moving* West, as it appears to remain alive and well in the East! And now an enhanced dialogue, exchange and transmission of energy continues. Where is it going through? It is going through the Mideast. So this dialogue, the receiving of all of this energy, these spiritual teachings, is coming not only from above, but it is also flowing from the East through the Mideast and on to the West. The West is also informing the East through the same channels. So an exchange is taking place. The Temple was meant to serve as a receiver and transmitter facilitating this exchange. It is a receiver and transmitter of this energy. The Jewish people, for whatever reason, were given the role to establish the Temple as a vehicle for the flow of that information, that message, back and forth.

In Eastern religion, there are many references to jewels, gems, diamonds. For example, there's the Diamond Sutra in Buddhism, and the Crest Jewel of Discrimination in Vedanta. In Yoga, the purified mind is likened to a gem, like a diamond. A diamond gets formed by geological pressures over millennia. Even then, when it is found in the rough, if you don't know what you're looking for, you probably wouldn't even recognize it. It needs refinement, polishing and human intervention to reach the state for its ultimate functioning. This reflects a theme of humans being "co-creators", being part of the Divine Plan, God's instruments on earth. We're here taking diamonds in the rough and doing what we need to do to make them these wonderful gems and crystals that can be used for all kinds of purposes. Diamonds are the ultimate, purest crystalline forms in the world, and possess crystalline transmittal powers. Consider this in light of the role of Judaism to set up a Temple and face it East, to be a receiver and transmitter. Consider that many of the diamonds that are bought and sold in the world go through Orthodox Jewish hands and go through Israel. It's an interesting connection.

America appears to be a significant culmination point for this process of transmission from the East. America, the New World, is the last stop. Despite all of our faults, our ideals of democracy, freedom and equality are still what the rest of the world aspires to. We're trying our best and we have our shortcomings, but we still stand as the standard-bearers for those ideals. And curiously, the United States contains the biggest concentration of Jewish people in the world, enjoying levels of freedom and prosperity unprecedented in their long history. A mere coincidence, a happenstance? Doubtful. The question and issue is, instead of the way it is being done now, how can those lofty aspirations somehow become spiritually infused so that they can be properly actualized? There is too much immature materialism in the West, and that is why the matured, perhaps over-ripe wisdom from the East is still being conveyed. It is needed to infuse that inner knowledge and convey that in addition to materialism, there also has to be a proper, deeper, perspective. That transmission is still necessary.

There is a rabbi with whom I have studied and for whom I have a great deal of respect. We once had an interesting dialogue. I asked him about the still prevalent conception found in traditional Orthodox Jewish teachings that we are the Chosen People, we are superior, we're this exclusive club, everyone else needs to acknowledge this and start following our lead. The descendents of Ishmael are our enemies, the descendents of Esau are our enemies. (Well, that's most of the world!) We are the best, we've got the inside track. There are smug, insider jokes about it. It is still a very common conception among Jewish people and how they talk among themselves. So I confronted this rabbi with my concerns that maybe there is little too much pride, that resentment is brewed from boasting and claims that we're the best, nobody else really matters — everyone else is supposed to come in step with us. He actually acknowledged that maybe we should tone it down and just quietly go about doing our business. Like everyone else, there's the proper business and the proper place for every group to function. Gloating causes problems. It has created resentment and persecution. Perhaps everyone would be better off if we all just went about taking care of our business, as it contributes to the betterment of the whole.

Connections Between Three Major Traditions: Judaism, Eastern Mysticism, Western Mysticism

There are three broad spiritual traditions through which I have been studying and operating. Yes, ultimately there is only one grand tradition. As has often been depicted to the point of cliché, there are many sides and paths to the one Truth at the top of the mountain. However, the paths can be, or at least appear to be, very distinct. A tradition at a certain level down the mountain has a lineage and a literature/scripture that is fairly unique to its tradition, distinct from other traditions that have their own lineages, teachings, practices and bodies of literature/scripture. Sometimes, they don't seem to overlap very much, although there may be some similarities. It would be helpful to provide an overview and perspective of my approach to the study of Judaism, based upon my exposure to these three traditions.

Judaism is the tradition of my birth. There is difficulty in getting a comfortable feel for Judaism because it is not only a religion, but it is also an ethnic identity, and now, because Israel is a Jewish nation, it is akin to a nationality. There are Jews all over the world. There are Jews that probably don't have a whole lot in common other than that somehow they all think they're Jews. Yet despite this diversity and dispersion all over the world, there has also been a remarkable consistency. Even though there is a wide variety of Jewish religious services, there are certain observances and holidays that are generally practiced and recognized by anyone who considers themselves a practicing Jew. There are certain common elements, whether it is Reform, Orthodox or Conservative or something else in between. There are common moral and ethical teachings and principles addressing relations with one's fellow man. There are bigger differences among the branches of Judaism in the realm of dogma, doctrine and ritual addressing one's relation to God.

There is also an aspect that there are many Jews that are not at all observant or "religious" in any common conception of those terms. They may observe the major holidays, but not much more. However, they still have a very deep identity as Jews. It is more an ethnic identity than a religious identity. Many people who are very supportive of Israel are hardly practicing Jews at all. They are relating to Jewish identity in a manner different than on a religious or spiritual level. It is like an Italian is an Italian, and proud to be an Italian. Most Italians are Catholics, but probably a lot of Italians hardly ever go to church. Well, a lot of Jews hardly ever go to synagogue, yet they still have a deep identity and relationship of being Jewish, and being proud to be Jewish. My family was like that. We didn't light Sabbath candles. We celebrated Hanukah with the blessings over the candles and the gift-giving, and we went to temple on the major holidays, but that was about it. We didn't keep kosher; we even ate bacon! However, we happened to live around the corner from a Modern Orthodox synagogue, and my parents wanted me to have somewhat of a Jewish religious training. If it had been a Reform temple around the corner, that would have been fine too. So out of happenstance and convenience I had a relatively Orthodox training as far as Hebrew School. I went three days a week for five years at two hours per session. From a kid's point of view, that was a major deprivation of my free time, preventing me from playing Little League baseball, which I resented but accepted. We learned quite a bit. However, it was inculcated from a certain simplistic fundamentalist point of view because kids can only conceive of so much. So my childhood training and Bar Mitzvah was through a perspective of what was designated a Modern Orthodox congregation, a shade more liberal than ultra orthodox.

Well, as I got a little bit older and I started thinking more on my own, many of those early childhood Hebrew School conceptions didn't make sense. In my teenage years, I went through my atheist period where I was rejecting all of that: the idea of the Big Daddy God up there and if you sin you'll be punished. If you dropped a Bible on the floor, you had to do things to make penance, not Hail

Marys, but other things. There were sins, and you felt guilty if you didn't go to temple because you knew you really were supposed to, things like that. So that is my basic Jewish upbringing and background.

In my searching for spirituality, as many others in my generation, I discovered and dabbled in Eastern thought, which I found very attractive, because the Western approaches weren't appealing to me. Western traditions seemed very dogmatic and external, while Eastern wisdom introduced the mysteries of fascinating inner realms. I had the benefit of studying Hinduism and Buddhism from a perspective of having had no background or upbringing within them or the cultures where they developed. By not having any of their cultural or ethnic filters and accompanying dogmas or biases, I could easily glean the pure spirituality in them, without getting caught up in their crystallizations. I eventually settled into this one particular yoga system that is called The Tradition of the Himalayan Masters. There is a lot more to yoga than what people think. The physical exercises are actually just one small part of yoga. That is part of it, but meditation to me is the core. I found that I was naturally a very meditative being. Vague, groping notions found clarification, definition and affirmation through my involvement with yoga and meditation. As I delved deeper through practices, classes and studying, it all started to make sense and gel. This particular tradition that I have been involved with for over thirty years is very broad and open-ended, allowing for a lot of flexibility. I was basically content with it, but every once in a while, I would wonder about Judaism. Am I supposed to do something with Judaism? Something would come along, and I would try it out, but I kept hitting dead ends. I finally resolved that the yoga and meditation approach was adequate in satisfying my spiritual needs. I'm not a religious person, I'm a spiritual person. I'm not into ritual or going to temple or church. Meditation and basing my life upon the precepts arising from it is the core for me. That is my particular predilection within the second tradition of yoga.

However, subtle, yet distinct messages kept whispering in my inner ear from within the yoga tradition: "Yes, you seem content here and you're fine with this, but you're also supposed to examine Judaism anew." As these messages persisted, I said, "Fine. If I'm supposed to be doing this, the best way for me to possibly get reinvolved with Judaism would be through Kabala, because I know that is mystical Judaism." I read a little bit about Kabala. You pick up one of those books or look it up in the *Encyclopedia Judaica*, you read a few sentences, and you say, "This is too much for me. I don't want to know. It is too involved, too complicated, too vast and intimidating. I don't want to deal with it." I said, "Well, that's the wrong way to go." Then I heard about this Center near where I live, in Atlanta, the Karin Kabalah Center. I went to an introductory lecture and discovered it had a Christian veneer. I was familiar and comfortable enough with Christian mysticism that it wasn't going to bother me as a Jew, as it would for many Jews. I was comfortable with how Christian mysticism related to Kabala was being presented at the Center. So I said, "All right, I'll do this." I went through the whole course, which is not an "instant karma", "instant enlightenment" consumer product. It is a two and a half year course of study employing extensive materials, thorough presentation and hands-on processes. The material and theoretical framework gets drilled into your head and your being if you stick to the program and engage in all of the suggested practices and exercises. As you take it step by step, it becomes a little less intimidating, less overwhelming. I know the names of all of the worlds and all of the Sephirot. I don't remember all of the colors, but I colored them at one point!

So this third major path, tradition, is what I refer to in a broad, sweeping manner, as the Western Mystical Tradition. There is a core from which a variety of traditions have stemmed, such as Theosophy, Jewish and Christian Kabala, Freemasonry, Rosicrucionism, and the work of Mark and Elizabeth Clare Prophet. Although there are some roots and connections with India and overlaps with traditional yoga, I still consider it a Western mystical tradition.

One particular offshoot from the Western Mystical Tradition that is incorporated into the lessons at the Karin Kabalah Center is called Agni Yoga. These were teachings that came through Nicholas and Helena Roerich, Russians who lived in the 20's and 30's. Like Helena Petronov Blavatsky before them, whose teachings generated Theosophy, their work and writings were based upon connection with "Mahatmas", certain higher beings who aid mankind. They traveled throughout Tibet, spent some time in America, but eventually settled in the Kulu Valley in the Himalayas for the latter portion of their lives. He was an artist, among other things.

In addition to several books and artwork, the Roerichs generated a series known as the Agni Yoga texts which came to them through the Mahatmas. There's a history behind these unusual and mysterious books, which you won't find in public bookstores. They are not promoted or intended for consumption by the general public. The Karin Kabalah director, Shirley Chambers, stumbled upon them and realized their significance in relation to what she was teaching. They were meant for an inner circle of people to discover and study, as Shirley did. The unusual manner in which they are written is not meant to address the intellect, but rather to *confound* it, so there is only limited value in trying to intellectually understand them. If you open up to them and the energy they are transmitting, they start having meaning and effects on non-intellectual levels. Once in a while, you can understand something that is said on an intellectual level, but it is hard to hold that meaning for very long, because these books are meant to address the unconscious.

The branch of the Western Mystical Tradition taught at the Karin Kabalah Center connected with the Jewish tradition because it incorporated Kabala, which had been developed by Jewish sources. However, after I finished that course, I was still being led to continue to examine the Jewish tradition. There remained little internal voices saying, "You need to do more." I said, "Fine, I'll try to do more." When I tried in the past, I'd pick up a book or explore this avenue or that avenue, but nothing clicked. This time around, I came across some books that sounded interesting, so I started reading one, I liked it, and it referred to others. For a while, I continued reading what I call these supplemental materials and eventually realized that they kept referring to the Torah. At some point, I realized that I had to stop focusing so much on the supplemental materials and begin an earnest study of the source, the Torah itself. I decided that I would align my study of Torah with the way that Jews do it all over the world, generally one section a week, completing one full reading on a predetermined schedule over the course of a year, and then starting over again. With some slight variations, Jews all over the world study the same portion during the same week, and I stepped in tune with them. I continue to do this, searching for different commentaries and angles. I've cycled through several times and also continue with the study of supplemental materials, both within and outside the Jewish tradition.

At some level, the various traditions seem very different. Yes, from a universalist point of view, they ultimately all express the same truth, but they appear to do so in different ways. However, the more I delved into it, I found more and closer connections. It was almost like they were all going up the same slope of the mountain instead of different sides. The remainder of this chapter provides examples of some of these connections.

"Tara" is one name for the Divine Mother in the Eastern Tradition, and "Torah" has some correlation, likewise encompassing the Feminine. One interesting thing about Biblical Hebrew is that if any words look alike, sound alike, appear alike, share the same amount of letters, same numerological values, there is usually some relationship between them. In Hebrew, each letter is a letter, a number, and a word. Our "b" is a "b", our "c" is a "c". But "bet" means "house" and the number "2", "gimel" means "camel" and the number "3". There is an elaborate numerology/gematria system of analysis and permutations that becomes mind-boggling, again with a correlate in the Indian tradition. One of the main philosophies in India besides Vedanta is Samkhya, which is considered the mother of mathematics. Jews likewise maintain that the Hebrew alphabet contains the essence of all mathematics.

The name of my primary spiritual teacher in the yoga tradition, who passed away in 1996, was Swami Rama. One of the books he wrote is *Living with the Himalayan Masters*. It contains his chronicles, his little stories about growing up. He had a very unique life. He was orphaned at a young age, and a Himalayan sage basically raised him as his own child. I'll just refer to him as "Swamiji", which is an honorific and a term of endearment used by people associated with a specific Swami. He had a master, the one who raised him, and his master had a master, both of whom were still living for some time while Swamiji was still living. Swamiji had an opportunity once or twice to visit that person whom he called his Grandmaster, his master's master, who mostly lived at high altitudes in Tibet. This lineage represented by these three generations are not just generations but are also hierarchical. What has come out is that Swamiji's master was working at the level of Sanatkumara. It's not clear what level his grandmaster was working at; that is hard to conceive if you have a sense of the level of functioning of Sanatkumara. Sanatkumara is a fuzzy figure in the Theosophical tradition of this highly evolved being beyond the level of the Ascended Masters/The Great White Brotherhood/The Mahatmas. He oversees a few beings below him who oversee the Ascended Masters. Then you have the Babaji that Shirley Chambers [the founder/director of the Karin Kabalah Center] has met, also known as Hariakhan Baba. According to Shirley and other sources, he was a more recent incarnation of another Hariakhan Baba who is referred to by Paramahansa Yogananda in his famous book, *Autobiography of a Yogi*. He is also referred to by Swamiji in his book, *Living With the Himalayan Masters*. The former Hariakhan Baba left his body in the 1920's but reappeared in another form in the 1970's. He is this eternal or close to eternal sage wandering around in the Himalayas and other areas. Swamiji has said that Hariakhan Baba, often referred to as "Babaji", another generic honorific, and Swamiji's master, commonly known as Bengali Baba, were fellow disciples of Swamiji's grandmaster and they were basically at the same level. So there is that fascinating connection, operating at these various levels of spiritual hierarchy.

In addition, according to Swamiji, Helena Petronov Blavatsky, HPB, the spiritual originator of Theosophy, studied directly with Swamiji's master. Now it is not clear if she was a Mahatma, because Swamiji's master was at a level beyond the Mahatmas, or if she was on the same level as Swamiji. Swamiji's tradition makes reference to "The Seven Sages", or "The Seven Rishis". My sense is that they are one and the same as the Mahatmas described in the Theosophical tradition, these highly advanced beings serving humanity. That is the level at which Swamiji was operating. So you have the Seven Sages, that are probably the same as the Mahatmas, you have Babaji and Swamiji's master operating at yet a higher level, and then there is Swamiji's grandmaster - who knows what level that is!

One point about spiritual hierarchy. When I first came across that terminology, I had an inherent dislike and resistance to it. It smacked of corporate structure and seemed to me to be inappropriate terminology for describing spiritual realms and beings. Levels of hierarchy generally denote levels of power and authority, even though accompanied by corresponding responsibility. Of course, in the spiritual realm, it also denotes levels of spiritual advancement and refinement. Nonetheless, it seemed to be too much of an ego-based power structure description for me to find palatable or be able to comfortably relate to. However, over the years, as I have been more exposed to it, I have come to appreciate not only the responsibility and refinement aspects, but that first and foremost, it is a *hierarchy of service*. These beings are not like temporal overlords collecting taxes and lording it over the lesser beings beneath them. They are *servants*, and by virtue of their advancement, their refinement, they are more in touch with their mission, more dedicated, devoted and aligned with their mission, which is service.

I discovered a possible connection between the Roerichs and Swamiji. Swamiji's book is called *Living with the Himalayan Masters* because he relays stories about growing up and studying with various masters. As part of Swamiji's training, his master would send him out to study with these other beings and report back to him, maintaining that it was not sufficient to study with only one person. Well, all of these other beings were connected anyway! They specialized in certain aspects, so he would be sent out to study their specialties. A good portion of the book narrates his meetings, experiences and lessons with these beings. It's not like he was a big name dropper, but he often identified by name many of the people with whom he studied, for example, Tagore, Gandhi, and many other great sages. However, it is interesting that there is one little section in the book where he doesn't refer to a particular person by name. Although there has been no one so far to confirm this, my feeling is that this little narration concerned his meeting Nicholas Roerich. It was an interesting description and chapter. Most of the chapters are short and fairly tightly organized, discussing one main event or theme. This chapter stands out in that it doesn't hold to this general design. It seems like it is uncharacteristically disconnected and wanders all over the place. In this chapter, entitled "At the Feet of the Masters", he talks about Babaji and his master's connection with Babaji, but he also makes a reference to meeting a "well-known painter from the West, and a Buddhist monk." One of Roerich's interests was Tibetan Buddhism, and I have a strong hunch that this painter was Roerich.

Early in Genesis, where the text is speaking about the Garden of Eden, there is a description of four rivers flowing out of the Garden. One is the Tigris, one is the Euphrates. There have been some issues about what the other two were, as they have names that do not correlate with any current or ancient names. One probably was the Nile. There's an opinion that the other one, called the "Pishon", was the Ganges. These are not far-out New Age interpretations; this is coming from traditional Jewish commentators. The Pishon/Ganges surrounded the land of "Havilah", believed to be a reference to India. Another fascinating description in the same section referring to the Pishon/Ganges and Havilah/India, refers to Havilah as a land of good gold, "bedolach" and "shoham stone". Jumping ahead to Exodus, where the text describes building the Mishkan, the portable Tabernacle in the desert which was the prototype for the permanent Temples later built in Jerusalem, and investing the High Priests, there is a lot of detail about the vestments of the High Priest. Part of the vestments was a breast plate. I initially had trouble envisioning the breast plate, because whenever I think of breast plate, I think of the knights of old, wearing their armor with a breast plate. But this was a breast plate for the High Priest. It was made of cloth, although there are issues about its composition. The main vestment on the main outer robe had a strap that came over each shoulder, and two more straps coming up from the waist. There were rings attached to each of the four straps. The breast plate was a square piece that was attached by its four corners to the rings. There were many items on the breast plate, including stones representing each of the twelve tribes and a stone for every letter in the Hebrew alphabet. The same shoham stones mentioned as coming from the land of Havilah/India in Genesis were included on the breast plate and the two shoulder straps attached to it.

Another interesting thing about this breast plate is that it wasn't just ornamental, it was functional. It was used for divination purposes, which is why it was called the "decision breastplate". When there was an important, weighty question, such as an issue of a war tactic, the High Priest would go into the inner chamber of the Holy of Holies wearing his full vestments, including the breast plate. He somehow posed the question to the Shekinah, the Divine Presence residing between the two Cherubim on the cover of the Ark, and he would come out with his breast plate lighting up. They would note the specific manner in which the breast plate was illuminating, spelling out answers, so it was used like an oracle. Again, this is not New Age fancy, it is right there in primary traditional sources. It was fascinating how the breast plate was used as an oracle, and that it contained shoham stones from India.

Do we know what exactly comprised the bedolach and shoham stones? When the text speaks of spices and gems and semi-precious stones, there is a problem that it often uses names with no known modern or ancient equivalent. Although there has been plenty of conjecture, no one is sure what they actually were, or what any ancient or modern equivalents might be. Conjecture about bedolach and the shoham stones ranges over a wide variety of gems or precious or semi-precious stones, including pearls and crystals. Concerning some materials with exotic names, some commentators claim that those substances no longer exist. Concerning the shoham, in my yoga tradition, there is a significant mantra called the "soham" mantra, meaning "that I am", "I am that". "Soham" certainly sounds a lot like "shoham". In fact, in biblical Hebrew, the same consonants would be used for the two words, with the only difference being the placement of a dot above the first letter, the Shin, which dot would serve more as a vowel and would not appear in the text which only contained consonants. I also get images of lingam stones in India, cylindrical stones made of various materials symbolizing the male sex organ, the male energy.

It has been a fascinating adventure to rediscover the Torah looking at it through new and fresh eyes. Until my new forays, my primary sources for Bible stories were things I remembered from my childhood and whatever is prevalent in popular culture. But there are many more Bible stories than I thought. There's the famous story of Abraham and Sarah. She was apparently barren and beyond child-bearing age, so she persuaded Abraham to have the child Ishmael through her servant Hagar. Then Sarah had her own miraculous conception and Isaac was born. What isn't very commonly known is that after all of the well-known events concerning Isaac and Ishmael, after Sarah died, Abraham remarried. Some authorities opine that he remarried the mother of Ishmael, Hagar, who at this later time is referred to as Keturah. One of the confusing things in the Torah is that many people have more than one name, with an alternative name often referring more to their function than a name. What is certain, and not conjecture, is that the main Torah text recites that after Sarah's death, Abraham took a wife named Keturah and had six more sons through that later marriage. There's an issue whether it was Hagar, the mother of Ishmael, but there is no issue about the fact that he had six sons after Isaac and Ishmael, and their names are provided in the main text.

An issue concerning Abraham's eight sons, as posed in the commentaries, is that at this juncture, God only wanted one lineal successor to carry on the work of Abraham, which was to be Isaac. There remain many issues concerning Ishmael, the Arab race descended from him, and the Muslim view on all of that, which is quite different than the Jewish view. But even in the Jewish view, Ishmael continued to live in the same geographic region as Isaac and they together buried Abraham. The Ishmael story in the Torah ends with his fathering a great nation and naming twelve successor sons, curiously the same number as Jacob's sons a generation later. As a matter of fact, Jacob's twin, Esau, married one of Ishmael's daughters. The main text clearly recites that Ishmael remained in the region and fostered a great multitude of prosperous nations of his own. Although there is nothing negative or derogatory about Ishmael or his descendants in the main Torah text, the standard Jewish commentators assign them such a spin. Abraham always felt for Ishmael. It was Sarah who insisted that Ishmael had to go. There is much discussion in the commentaries about all of that. But just reading it on its face, there was nothing negative or derogatory in the Torah text itself about Ishmael. It was all positive. He had his own generations. Yes, he was the son of a maidservant, but four of the tribes of Israel were sons of maidservants too, and there are hardly any issues raised about that.

All we know about Abraham's other six sons is that he sent them to the East with his "gifts", never to be referred to again in the main Torah text. As noted above, Ishmael and his descendants are discussed, and Isaac becomes the lineal successor to Abraham's mission, which, according to the commentators, included the bequest to Isaac of all of Abraham's material and spiritual wealth, except for these "gifts" which were sent off to the East with the other six sons.

There has been some conjecture about these other six sons in secondary sources. There are recognized Jewish sources who have explicated that these gifts were not mere material items and valuables; rather, these involved mastery of occult mystical powers and meditation techniques. According to these traditional Jewish sources, these six sons of Abraham became six of the seven ancient ancient Rishis/Sages of India. Again, this is from traditional Jewish sources, not some far-flung "new age" conjecture. It backs up the claim that Judaism came first, and that they are the ones who were masters of meditation. These six sons of Abraham were taught meditation and became six of the seven ancient Vedic Rishis of India, where they promulgated the meditative arts that emerged out of the Indian Vedic tradition. However, my yoga tradition mentions *Seven* Sages, suggesting the possibility that perhaps they encountered and joined forces with someone who was already there. Apparently there is this *seventh* sage who isn't accounted for in the Jewish rendition, because there were six of these sons. Although this has been conveyed more as conjecture than confirmed fact, a vague source from within my Yoga tradition suggests that Moses was actually an incarnation of one of the ancient Vedic sages. Coupling this idea with the above Jewish notion about Abraham's sons leads to the conclusion that Moses was an incarnation of one of the sons of Abraham, if not of this seventh sage. In typical fashion supporting the superiority of their system, the Jewish sources make derogatory comments that the gifts given to the six sons were of lesser occult powers, they misused them in India, and they became debased and distorted.

Abraham gave the pure, advanced methods to Isaac, while these six sons got the second rate stuff and took it to India. Jewish sources have difficulty refraining from belittling anything other than their truth.

Another pretty obvious connection between the Kabala tradition and the Yoga tradition is the relationship between the description of the chakras in the yoga system, seven primary energy centers depicted as discs/wheels/spheres running from the base of the spine to the top of the head, and the Tree of Life with the three pillars and the Sephirot in the Kabala system, where there are similar centers of energy depicted as spheres connecting the bottom to the top, also correlated with the human body. In Yoga, there is a middle channel and two side channels of energy as in the Kabala system. A difference is that Yoga doesn't break it out and describe any centers on the side channels the way that Kabala does. However, if you count each of the three pairs of the side Sephirot as one unit, with their energies balanced in the middle, the result is the same number of seven as in yoga (the three side pairs plus the four on the middle pillar. Please see the illustrations at the end of Chapter Four). The focus in both systems is to balance the two side channels and ascend up the central channel, while at the same time, imploring the bestowing descent of Grace from above. In both systems, the top center is called the Crown and the center in the middle of the chest is called the Heart. Another difference is in Kabala, the lowest Sephirah is usually described as corresponding with the feet, while in yoga, it corresponds with the base of the spine. However, in yoga meditation, you traditionally sit cross-legged, with the heals of the feet in close proximity to the base of the spine, which may explain this discrepancy.

Yet another significant connection between Yoga and Judaism is the symbol of the Jewish Star. What is commonly referred to as "The Jewish Star" existed before Judaism. The Jewish Star is the traditional symbol in the Yoga system for the Heart Center. Swamiji in *Living with the Himalayan Masters* has referred to Jews as being "meditators on the Star of David". There are *mantras* emanating from inner sound, and there are also something called *yantras*, emanating from inner sight. You can meditate on sounds and you can meditate on images, contemplate visual depictions. One of the significant images in the Yoga system comprises a geometric extension off of the basic Jewish Star called the Sri Yantra or Sri Chakra. It is maintained that deep spiritual insight into comprehending this image results in enlightenment. There are techniques for contemplating this image in order to penetrate its spiritual depth. It is said that the meaning and energy of all of the chakras are contained in this one image.

So there are a lot of connections.

36

Chapter Two

Layers Upon Layers
Major Themes
Another Take on Exile

Layers Upon Layers

The study of Judaism, the study of Torah, involves layers. It's been refreshing for me to approach this from a whole new angle, having been away from it for so long, after being immersed in the intervening years in yoga and meditation, and then coming back to Torah and Judaism. I've been like a kid in a candy store, seeing these things from a whole new point of view, in a whole different light. It's been a lot of fun. I have a revelation, an insight, and then I discover that someone else, often-times hundreds of years ago, has already had that same revelation or insight. But that's okay because I had it before I discovered that somebody else already had it, and it fosters a wonderful sense of the continuity and tradition of Torah study. Below are entries from my spiritual journal concerning this process and the impact it has had on me. I advise keeping a spiritual journal, because it is a practice that is beneficial to your spiritual growth. These are a couple of selections illustrating the process of studying Torah and Judaism and its impact, providing a flavor of a revelation I had, and then how I found it elsewhere:

"I have undertaken the practice of reading the weekly Torah portion, accompanying Haftorah, and commentary from The Stone Edition and The Living Torah. While doing so one day recently, I had a flash of insight. It actually might not appear to be a new idea, but the depth of understanding of this insight was what was new for me. I had this realization that the words I was reading, the physical Torah and its written words, were nothing more than an elaborate book cover. There was something underneath it much more vast, powerful and meaningful than the Torah itself. The Torah itself was just a veneer, an external wrapping. The question was, what lay beneath the veneer, for that was the real Torah. The veneer, the wrapping, and all that it posed, was just a material entry portal. In the days that followed this flash of insight, the nature of this insight deepened further to a generalization about life and what we call the material

world. I could see more clearly how the material world is just a crystallization, a congealing of energies meeting within a specific matrix, that there are other worlds and realities from which these energies come to congeal temporarily here, and there are other worlds and realities to which these energies are going after their expression through this particular matrix. Energies from other dimensions converge and intermingle to create this three-dimensional world. I saw the mathematical aspect to this, as this matrix of the material world is just like a three-dimensional Cartesian plane/cube. I could see how theoretical mathematics could analyze and describe this matrix, and inquire into the mechanics of the other worlds from which these energies come and to which they will be traveling."

Soon after that, I had a dream. I get a lot of teachings through dreams. Sort of a sexy dream, but here it is, nonetheless. It follows up on the above:

"I was visiting an art studio, and there was a painting by a particular female artist that caught my attention. [Female is interesting, because Torah is related to creation, and anything in creation is female, form]. It was of a reclining nude female, shown from the waist up. There was a certain seductiveness to it, but also a certain aloofness/indifference. It was as if to say, 'I am here and available if you like, but if you don't, I don't really care.' There was a light in the frame which appeared to be there just to illuminate the painting. I then noticed some type of image at the right side of the figure, and then images began appearing throughout the painting. At first I thought I had just missed seeing them at first blush, and that on closer inspection, I noticed them. But then I realized that the painting was transforming, that these other images were bleeding through, as if from a deeper layer that was coming through to the surface. Eventually, the painting transformed to a totally different scene, and then the same process began again, with images from yet a third layer/scene beginning to bleed through until again a totally new scene appeared. This process kept happening about ten times. I realized that this was a special technological process, and that the light at the top was part of the transforming technology. [Light − isn't that interesting]. It was very fascinating and captivating.

"In contemplating this dream today, it became apparent to me that this was a depiction of the Torah. As I believe I have said in an earlier entry, I have begun the process of studying the weekly Torah portion. I first read the portion and comments from the Stone Edition, and then I read the same portion from The Living Torah by Aryeh Kaplan. I believe this process is having a deep effect upon

me. I recall my last session with Panditji [my spiritual teacher from the yoga tradition] over New Years, in which he told me that there is an association between Mt. Kailash in Tibet and Mt. Sinai, as if Mt. Kailash manifested as Mt. Sinai. He also told me that there is an association between the word 'Torah' and the word 'Tara', which is one of the names of the Divine Mother. In the Torah section I read this weekend, the first detailed specifications for the Ark and Tabernacle are given. The cover for the Ark contains two Cherubim, one male and one female, and God told Moses that he would come and speak with Moses from between the two Cherubim. The commentary related this Divine Presence to be that of the Shekinah, which is generally depicted as the Female aspect of Divinity, similar to the Divine Mother or Kundalini.

"As I said in an earlier entry, it became clear to me that the written Torah was like an involved cover to a book, and that the book itself lay in layers within. There are layers upon layers to this revelation of Truth. It seemed like the depiction in the painting was the surface depiction of the Divine Mother/The Shekinah, which gave way to the inner layers that came forth as attention remained focused on the painting".

So I had these revelations and it felt pretty cool. Soon thereafter, I entered into an email dialogue with a Chabad rabbi with whom I have been studying. This is an interesting part of a response he gave to a question I posed to him: "The Torah as we know it is already brought down to a human finite level of understanding. In its Divine source it is obviously far more intense, as it comprises spiritual rather than a physical component. Take, for example, the words that are spoken from the human mouth. They are intellectual thoughts processed for distribution. In their origin, however, they are far more intense and contain far more energy than the simple words that contain the knowledge that is expressed. In that vein, the first monotheists up until the time of Sinai accessed the Torah on a spiritual level. For example, the mitzvah of tefillin didn't have a box and straps on it. Rather, it contained the energy of intellect over emotion, as is represented by the hand tefillin and the head tefillin. [The Shema prayer contained in the Torah has a passage that contains the mitzvah/commandment to bind the words of the Torah on the arm and hold them between the eyes. This evolved into the orthodox Jewish practice of wearing little boxes containing selected portions of scripture, secured by leather straps, to the arm and the forehead during weekday prayer. These boxes are called tefillin or phylacteries. I've come across other sources substantiating the idea that the real tefillin are inside, and what is seen and worn are just external representations.] Ultimately, though, the intention is for us to observe the Torah in a physical manner. And thus the Torah was given at Sinai in a tangible physical way." He is relaying that there are internal layers, but it also needs to be externally expressed. We are placed here in the material world to perform the ultimate, culminating expression. That is the explanation for his orthodox observances. He's a Chabad Lubavitcher Hasidic Jew, and they are supposed to do every single last little thing that is possible to do in religious observance in the physical world. It has origins way back, but we're still supposed to be expressing all of this in the physical world today.

I then started reading a book containing a synopsis of sections of the Zohar. The real Zohar consists of multiple volumes, and is considered one of the primary written sources for Jewish mysticism and Kabala. I came across this famous quote from the Zohar on the hidden meaning of Torah: "Woe to the sinners who look upon the Torah as simply tales pertaining to things of the world, seeing thus only the outer garment. But the righteous whose gaze penetrates the very Torah, happy are they. Just as wine must be in a jar to keep, so the Torah must be contained in an outer garment. That garment is made up of the tales and stories. But we, we are bound to penetrate beyond." (From *Zohar, The Book of Splendor, Basic Reading from the Kabalah*, Edited by Gershom Scholem).

So obviously, other people have had my revelation about layers and deeper meanings. That's what I'm interested in learning and conveying. The externalizations are at times hard to penetrate, particularly if you've been brought up and taught as a child in a tradition. That's when people start rejecting what they've been taught. As they grow up they start examining and rejecting all of the over-simplified child-oriented representations, and may even go through an atheist period like I did. Hopefully, you eventually return and discover that there is more to it. There are a lot of levels.

Major Themes

A question that I have pondered is, "What are the themes that are being addressed in Torah study?" In Judaism, there is a big tradition of study, study, study. One of the main practices in Judaism is that the Torah - and here I mean the Torah in the narrower sense of the Five Books of Moses - is divided into weekly sections, which total 54, so that with some manipulations for weeks when a section isn't read, and accommodation for those years in the Jewish calendar when there is an extra month, the entire Torah, the Five Books of Moses, is read and studied, section by section, week by week, every year. The centerpiece of a traditional Jewish Saturday Sabbath service is the reading of the weekly portion. So every year, week by week, Jews go through one reading of the entire Torah, and then start over again. To me, that is part of some function that Jews are meant to be doing. They're bringing that energy down to earth and grounding it here. That is one of the roles that they're to perform, not just for themselves, but for the betterment of all humankind. Every Saturday everywhere in the world on the Jewish Sabbath, with some slight variations, that same Torah portion is being chanted in synagogues and temples all over the world. And the Torah portion is not only to be chanted/read, it is supposed to be studied. In addition to observances incorporating emotional elements, Judaism has also always emphasized the intellectual side. Study, study, study.

It seems that there are a few main themes to all of this studying, praying, and grounding of energy. Judaism, as with most religions, includes a deified aspect of the Divine, with Judaism claiming that it was the first religion to establish *monotheism*, the conception that there is one all-encompassing Deity without a second. "Theism" means an embodiment, a personification, a deification, an anthropomorphism of this Divine Entity somehow separate from me the poor slob sitting here. Yoga distinguishes "monotheism" and "monism". Yoga teaches that there is an impersonal unity underlying everything, the *Brahman* behind everything, beyond Deification. So there is *monism*, and there is *monotheism*. The monotheistic emphasis of Judaism, as in most western traditions, has dwelled upon this conception that there is man and woman, human being and all other beings and elements of creation, and then there is God, separate and apart. Although God is Ominpresent, Omniscient and Omnipotent, at some significant level, God and creation are not the same; they're different and separate. We are here to try to understand and worship God and do what God tells us to do the best we can and follow His commandments. One aspect of study is about trying to better understand and establish an individual's relationship with the Divine. If we have a theistic Deity that we call God, what is our relationship with that entity? A second aspect addresses an individual's relationship with everybody and everything else in creation that appear as entities separate from the Divine and the individual. If we are separate from God and separate from other elements of creation, how do we relate with everything else in the world? One analysis of the Ten Commandments notes that half of them address our relationship with God and the other half address our relationship with our fellow human beings and our world around us.

Another theme concerns the connections between this Deified Entity, us and our world. How is all of that interfacing? What is the interrelationship between all of these? You find this inquiry more developed in mystical aspects of Judaism and Kabala. There's an interesting representation concerning "Divine Sparks". Kabalistic/mystical Judaism suggests that everything in creation, animate and inanimate, contains a Divine Spark. That Divine Spark may be embedded very deeply within an entity that we perceive as a separate thing or being. These Divine Sparks are spread everywhere. Part of the role of a Jew is to make a connection with and enliven those Divine Sparks. The Divine Sparks provide the opportunity to establish a connection between Divinity and the world around us. There are personal and impersonal aspects to this process. The personal aspect is that each individual – this incorporates some conception of 'soul-mates' or the 'six degrees of separation' or things like that – that each individual has certain souls, certain Divine Sparks spread out over the world that have a closer, particular connection with that individual. Part of our goal and reason for living is to try to establish those connections. They in turn will enliven us, and we in turn will enliven them and make those Divine Sparks grow. There is also a more impersonal universal aspect that wherever they are, whether there's a particular closer personal connection or not, we're supposed to seek out these Divine Sparks and help enliven them. That is part of the role of human beings, to connect with the Divine Sparks that are spread everywhere.

Another theme in Judaism that some have tied into the concept of the Divine Sparks concerns the long history of persecution and dispersion, what is called the "Diaspora," "Galut," "Exile". Accompanying this is the idea of an eventual return to wholeness, a redemption, usually tied to the rebirth of a Jewish nation in Israel heralded by the Messiah and the rebuilding of the Temple in Jerusalem. There is a positive mystical take on the Diaspora related to the conception of the Divine Sparks, most prominently espoused by Isaac Luria, an extremely influential proponent of Kabala within Judaism. There is this image that the world is in some way broken, akin to being a broken vessel. The pieces are scattered all over. The goal of spiritual life is to gather these pieces together and make them whole again. One of the reasons for this "galut", this exile, this dispersion, and the destruction of the Temples, was that the Jewish people needed to go out and enliven these sparks of Divinity that are hidden and concealed throughout the world, to collect these scattered broken pieces of the vessel to help make it whole again. There is a related concept called "tikkun", meaning "to make whole", "to make complete". Part of the mission of the Jewish people is to bring things to completion. Wherever we go and whatever we do, we're supposed to be looking for these sparks to enliven and liberate, to collect these broken pieces of the vessel to bring them back together, repair it and make it whole. The exile, which seemed like such a horrible thing to happen, was intended to spread people throughout the world to do that. Another side benefit of dispersion is that it makes the total genocide of the Jewish people difficult, if not impossible.

Another theme concerns the concept of expressing Divinity on earth. You find this emphasized by sources such as Shirley Chambers [as you may recall, the teacher of Christian Kabala at the Karin Kabalah Center, with whom I have studied] and the Roerichs [as you also may recall, Nicholas and Helena Roerich were a Russian couple who lived and taught in the first half of the 20th century]. Human life should be focused on expressing Divinity and Beauty on earth. For the Roerichs, art was a significant form for such expression. Art in its purest form is Divine expression through human agency. We can turn our entire lives and everything we do into works of art. It doesn't have to be a traditional expressive work of art. What we're here to do, as participants and co-creators in this physical existence, is to express this Beauty just for the sake of it. Judaism teaches, as others do, that God created the universe because God wanted to express Himself/Herself/Itself; we're here to help express, elevate, energize Divinity. It goes back to the cliche of "Performing senseless acts of beauty and random acts of kindness". Judaism expresses that we're here to "bring heaven down to earth". It goes both ways: we're here both to elevate earth to heaven and to bring heaven down to earth. That's what we're here for.

So those are some basic overarching themes addressed in Judaism. You may have an impression that this is far out, "new age" Judaism. But this is actually fairly traditional Judaism rooted in traditional sources, sages and commentaries. It is just not talked about very much. If you go and study it, you will find it. True, some may be Kabalistic, mystical perspectives from time immemorial that were traditionally not supposed to be revealed to the common person. The tradition had generally been that only married men over forty years old, after a rigorous course of preliminary study, might begin to be divulged these kind of teachings. However, now more and more recognized sources, rabbis and teachers within the tradition are beginning to open up. These days, you can find it on the Internet! But again, these are not just crazy fringe new age kind of people or teachings. This is primary source material.

A continuing issue involved in a study of Judaism, as is true with most religious study, concerns the distinction between the literal and the figurative. There are sources that support a point of view that Israel doesn't necessarily have to be a physical place. Israel is a state of being. We're involved with layers upon layers and levels upon levels. One emphasis that is frequently made in Judaism and in other traditions is that the material world is the culmination, the end point of everything. The entire process that is graphically portrayed in the Kabalistic scheme of the four worlds and the four trees of life indicates the end point of all of these subtle machinations is Malkuth of Assiyah, the material world here on earth. So there is particular significance to the physical world and physical expression. The traditional Jewish point of view acknowledges the symbolism, but also emphasizes the literal.

For example, the physical design of the Temple on earth mirrors the design of the Temple in another world. The earthly Temple is a physical congealing of the other-worldly energies. But it was meant to be physical because we've been put here in the physical world to accomplish this. We were put here to build this physical Temple. We can go into all kinds of discussions as to why it was destroyed. It was destroyed once and rebuilt. It was destroyed a second time. The period between the first two wasn't all that long, 570 years. Now it has been two thousand years. Only very recently, the State of Israel has been reinstituted. So there's a lot of excitement about when the new Temple is coming. For many people within Judaism, and certainly the more orthodox, the fundamentalists, there will be a physical rebuilding of the Third Temple on the site of the others. The same kind of activities that were conducted in the past Temples will be reinstituted again: investiture of a High Priest and attendants, conducting all of the commandments about the sacrifices, burnt offerings, slaughtering and butchering of animals and the infrastructure to convey the blood out of the Temple and return it to the earth. I can't imagine it myself. I think that is how it is supposed to be, but in a very different manner than is commonly conceived, as discussed more fully in the next chapter.

Another Take on Exile

As noted above, one important theme underlying Jewish history, and thus collective Jewish experience, is that of exile and its accompanying struggle and suffering. Adam and Eve are exiled from the Garden, the Jewish people are exiled in Egypt, the Babylonian Captivity followed by the Roman destruction of the Second Temple and its resultant dispersion and assimilation of the Jewish people, the Holocaust tragedy at the hands of Hitler while in exile, and today identified Jews live exiled from their homeland Israel, and the descendants of ten of the twelve tribes remain yet unidentified. There is the suffering in the knowledge of being away from Home, the suffering of living as outsiders in others' lands with its accompanying ostracism and persecution, and the struggle to establish Home and insure its continued existence.

All too often, literal fact, literal history, is seen only literally. External events are viewed only externally and assigned only superficial meaning. However, external events may hold significant lessons concerning one's own internal condition and be only a reflection of more subtle events taking place within each of us individually and all of us collectively. This type of interpretation should also be emphasized in attempting to understand the meaning of our history and religion.

We are here to learn, to discover, uncover, recover. In order to understand that which occurs outside, we must develop and understand that which occurs

44

inside. Our ability to understand the outside world is limited by our understanding of our inner selves. The inner self is the tool through which the outer world becomes known. Ignore the tool, remain the fool, so to speak.

All the events of the external world, the macrocosm, can be seen as elements within each individual's internal world, their microcosm. Our perceptions, opinions, actions, and reactions concerning external events are reflections of our internal states. A self-analysis of the manner in which we interact with the external world is useful in understanding our inner workings. The reason for this analysis is to Know. The reason for Knowing is to expand our ability to enjoy life, to be a positive force in life, and to find Ultimate Meaning.

There is a great Dilemma we all face, which centers on the problem that just as there is darkness and pain in the external world, there is also darkness and pain in the internal world. Many people base their lives on developing means to minimize external pain and maximize external pleasure. This superficial quest for fulfillment in the external world is doomed to failure because pain can never be totally avoided, as all things external are superficial and not permanent. External pleasures are limited in scope and durability, and their inevitable loss results in pain and a renewed neurotic attempt to attain new pleasures which again won't last. Attaining the commonly-accepted conditions of external success most often has little bearing on a sense of true inner fulfillment, and may create hindrances to inner satisfaction.

The Dilemma we face is that a more lasting fulfillment can only be attained by going within and truly understanding the basis of one's existence on the most subtle of inner levels; but the pain and darkness which must be encountered and overcome on an internal quest is much greater and more profound than that in the external world. And the path to inner fulfillment is strewn with unavoidable unpleasantness which must be encountered and overcome, not avoided. So most of us choose instead not to engage in such a quest because of the intense fear we have of our own internal unknown. It is the only path to ultimate, lasting fulfillment, but it is too frightening to undertake, and thus our dilemma. Instead, most of us tend to carry on and act out our internal yearning, our internal turmoil, in the external world where attempts at true fulfillment are doomed to fail.

Now what does this have to do with Judaism's theme of exile, you may ask. Well everything, I answer. The true meaning of exile is exile from oneself. We struggle and suffer because we are separated from our own true Selves, from our inner source of ultimate strength and nurturance. Jews (and others) have a great tendency to look at the external world and point at others and circumstances beyond their control for the source of their suffering and their exile. No one wants to consider that the true home land, Israel, is a state of being, not a plot of land in the Middle East or anywhere else. And the true source of suffering, the basis of our exile, is self-inflicted, not other-inflicted. We turn away from our Source, our homeland, rather than towards it. We breed separation in the external world - us/them, good guys/bad guys - which in turn only breeds and deepens our internal separation from our true Selves. The external bad guys are only reflections of our own negative tendencies, limited viewpoints, and fears. It is much easier and more consoling to point our fingers at others and do battle with them than to confront the violence and turmoil which exists within ourselves. Yet it remains our most important and profound duty to undertake the torturous trek towards our true and everlasting Home which resides within - to confront and overcome the dangers and obstacles of our own ignorance, weakness, and fear. Only then can real Fulfillment be realized.

Just as the external world has light, which is the ultimate source of nurturance in the external world, so does the internal world have light as its ultimate source of nurturance. If there is some conscious awareness of the inner light, it can be focused and intensified. By focusing on the inner light, it is possible to confront and overcome internal turmoil and fear, for this light guides us towards Home, to its Source, and provides the strength and sustenance needed along the way.

Chapter Three

Jacob and Esau

[Note: For those unfamiliar with the stories or personages referred to in the main text, please see the section in the Appendix entitled "Summary of Torah Events and Personages"]

In the traditional Jewish commentaries, the descendants of Esau are Western Europeans, descended from the ancient Romans and others. This traditional thought, still propagated today, also holds that Esau is a sworn enemy of the children of Jacob until Messiah comes. I confronted a rabbi about this, because my reading is that most of the white Western European world that now exists are all descendants of Esau. His response was that all of that is just figurative, that it is the Esau *nature* that we're enemies with, not the physical descendants. But if you read some of the commentaries, they seem to be speaking pretty literally, going to great pains to illustrate the lines of descent from Esau into the various modern white Western nationalities. That's a tough pill to swallow if taken literally. When being literal gets too uncomfortable it becomes only figurative. A big issue is, who is determining what is to be taken literally, or only figuratively?

There is an interesting alternative take on Esau that can also be found in the traditional commentaries. One analysis is that Jacob and Esau had an opportunity to establish a harmonious balance between the left and right sides of the Kabalistic Tree of Life. They represented different aspects, and if their varying natures had been properly blended, their merging could have established a holistic civilization, a perfected whole earth Tree way back at that time. But something happened so that didn't quite work out. One view is that it was intended for Esau to wed Leah instead of Jacob. When that didn't occur, possibly due to Leah's recalcitrance, there remained an opportunity for Esau to wed Jacob's daughter Dinah, but Jacob hid Dinah from Esau.

There are different interpretations about Esau, his energy, what he meant, what he was. However, the most prevalent conception of Esau found in traditional commentaries is that his descendants are the sworn enemies of the descendants of Jacob. Many of the persecutors of the Jewish people over the centuries were not stark barbarians. They were educated and knowledgeable about what the Jews were teaching to each other. Such teachings are inevitably going to breed resentment. The gentile response to the Jews is, "You're saying we're your sworn enemy for all of eternity. And besides that, you killed our Messiah." What's going on here?

There is something to learn from history, and although it is okay to have a certain pride in your heritage, there remain issues of reinterpreting or choosing which interpretation to emphasize. Even within the traditional commentaries, there exist kernels of a more positive interpretation concerning Esau which run contrary to the common interpretation. There are parallel alternatives concerning the role of the serpent in the Garden of Eden. One symbol for Pharaoh was a serpent. The serpent was Evil and enticed Man to exercise his Evil Inclination (Jewish view), or was the cause of Original Sin (Christian view). But there is another connotation and way of looking at it more in line with the yoga conception of the Kundalini Shakti, the Serpent Power, as a positive and necessary element required for creation to express. This power, in and of itself, is neutral, but in the case of Pharaoh, it got misused. Again there is the issue of which interpretation gains prominence and which one gets lost. All religions get convoluted over time and need to be refreshed, renewed. That is the principle espoused by the Jewish Renewal movement, emphasizing an infusion of dynamic, evolutionary *renewal*, as distinguished from the static, dogmatic attempts at *restoration* by the traditional Orthodox.

Egypt the Mother

The general Jewish commentaries portray Egyptian society at the time of Moses as the most depraved society that the earth has ever known, consistent with a long-standing negative Jewish attitude towards Egypt. However, there has been an incredible symbiotic relationship between Egypt and Israel throughout history. Abraham, Jacob, Moses and Jesus all went there. Maimonides, one of the most respected of all the Middle Age Jewish authorities, moved to and lived in Egypt. He was a physician to leading Egyptian dignitaries. His works and commentaries that are widely cited were all written in Arabic. In Alexandria, there was a thriving Jewish community. Isaac Luria, the father of modern Kabbalah, lived in Egypt for a good deal of his life. Despite this remarkably positive relationship, Jews have persisted in regarding Egypt in a derogatory fashion, and then they wonder why there is resentment.

You can see this astounding relationship between Israel and Egypt by their physical representations on a map. Egypt is the mother of Israel. Abraham's visit marked the insemination. The captivity as the result of Joseph and Jacob going there was the gestation. The Exodus under Moses was the birth. Physically looking at the map, you have the narrow Nile valley comparable to a birth canal, and out of it emerges the Jewish people. The Hebrew word for Egypt is "Mitzrayim", which means "narrowness". The waters that broke were the Red Sea, resulting in a birth into a new land and realm of promise, the land of Israel. Even physically looking at the land of Israel, the shape of it is almost a human shape, as if it had emerged out of a birth canal, the Nile valley, of its mother, Egypt. Maybe there is a reason why of all of the nations in the Middle East today, Egypt is the one that has made the most inroads towards recognizing and establishing peace with Israel. Food for thought.

The Seven Canaanite Nations

Another interesting aspect and insight/revelation that struck me concerns the seven Canaanite nations that were residing in the Promised Land at the time of the Exodus from Egypt. After the Hebrews had left Egypt and were ready to enter the Promised Land, they were to conquer the seven Canaanite nations. There have always been issues concerning interpreting the text. Did it really mean to conquer and totally obliterate them, or did it only mean to exercise dominion over them, but it was okay if they lived? There have been issues raised over the fact that they did not totally obliterate them. One point of view is that because of this, many things did not work out right, including the destruction of both Temples. Another point of view is that the Israelites were not supposed to totally obliterate them, that's not the proper meaning or translation. As long as those nations committed to follow the Seven Noachide Laws (see the Appendix), it was acceptable for them to coexist in the same land.

In any event, in the Torah, there is a directive to conquer the seven Canaanite nations. It came to me in a flash of insight as I was studying this through the eyes of my Yoga tradition that I saw a connection with the seven main chakras (energy centers) in the human body described in the yoga system. I had already conceived of the images discussed above, of Egypt having given birth to Israel and how the shape of the country of Israel resembles a human body. Then here comes a description of seven Canaanite nations existing within this bodily form. The Israelites are told by their God to enter the land and conquer the seven Canaanite nations. Well, the scheme in Yoga is that the chakras are energy centers along the spine, appearing to have a correspondence to the Sephirot on the Kabala Tree of Life, as discussed earlier in Chapter One. One definition of Yoga is "union", also coming from the root word for "yoke". Yoga involves yoking, controlling, exercising dominion over these energies for one's well-being and spiritual development. To conquer the chakras is not to destroy them, but rather to place their energy under your control. The idea is that once you become familiar with the energy levels of your chakras and you gain control over them so that they're not controlling you, they begin to function together at a higher level of harmony and internal integration. It is similar to the conception of a perfected Tree of Life in Kabala. You're a realized human being, you're a realized yogi, because you have encountered and exercised dominion over these inner forces that if not harmonized, create inner discord. You have *conquered* your seven chakras. They continue to exist and function because they are essential to life. You're not *obliterating* them, you're *harmonizing* them. Sometimes in yoga they say you have to destroy the ego. You don't really *destroy* the ego, you *control* the ego by reducing its common bloating and putting it in its proper place. The same goes for the chakras. You need to control them and put them under your dominion so you're in charge, not them. It dawned on me that perhaps the seven Canaanite nations are meant to be symbolic of the seven chakras. There's plenty of food for thought and research as how they might be related to the chakras. What was each of their names? What kind of characteristics did each one of them have?

This interpretation can have a bearing on the ongoing issues concerning who should live in and control Palestine, and whether there can be co-existing Jewish and Palestinian states. Perhaps the descendants of the seven Canaanite nations are supposed to be there. They're supposed to live and work in accord with the Jews that are there. It's not for them to kick the Jews out and push them into the sea, and it's not for the Jews to insist that they go live somewhere else or treat them as second class citizens. They're both supposed to live there in harmony. Perhaps the Third Temple, however it is supposed to come about, isn't going to be established until these matters are resolved. Perhaps this viewpoint warrants some consideration. For me, it has been a revelation, a new way of seeing things, a new possibility.

Even though there remain numerous difficulties in the Mideast, there appears to be some movement from both sides. There are definitely Palestinians who want to live peaceably with Jews; there are definitely Jews who want to live peaceably with Palestinians. Maybe it is a long way off. I think this model of a symbiotic relationship between the peoples is a new and promising way to see it. There is a correlation to the stories of Jacob and Esau and Isaac and Ishmael. Jacob and Esau are actually supposed to work harmoniously together; they're not supposed to be eternally sworn enemies. Likewise for Ishmael and Isaac. The idea is that there is always polarity and duality, but they're different sides to the same coin. They need to work together.

Modern Times

There are no High Priests now. There are rabbis now, and there's a big distinction between the two. During the times of the Temples, there was a definite hierarchy. There was a High Priest, assistant Priests and Levites serving the Temple; there was the Sanhedrin, which was the religious, civil and criminal court all rolled into one; and there were the yeshivas, which were academies of learning with their own hierarchies. There were religious, judicial, legislative, executive and academic authorities. Once the second Temple was destroyed, the hierarchy that went along with it was destroyed. There are a lot of issues in Judaism in the post-Temple period. The Orthodox emphasize that until the early 1800's, although there were always degrees and grades within Judaism, it was all sort of Orthodox. Other than a significant split for a while between the traditional Orthodox establishment and the upstart Hasidic movement that began in the 1700's, within a certain range of variation, the practices and observances were basically Orthodox. The differences were never discordant or severe enough to define denominations, or *movements* or *branches*, which are terms preferred over the term "denominations", as you find now. The movement which originated Reform Judaism, and spurred the various other movements that followed, started in the 1820's. The Conservative movement came next, and then we have all of these others: Modern and Neo-Orthodox, Traditional, Jewish Renewal and Reconstructionism. The history and differences between the various movements are described in more detail in the Appendix.

So the basic Orthodox conception is that when the Temple doesn't exist, the hierarchy is gone. It's a little questionable as to who has the ultimate authority for anything. The Hasidic movement addressed this authority vacuum to some extent. They had "Rebbes", as distinct from *rabbis*, who were acknowledged wise and experienced men, who served as more than just teachers; they served a similar function as gurus serve in the yoga tradition. Mystical powers and miraculous events are associated with them, along with the ability to effectuate deep spiritual transformation, catharsis and epiphanies within individuals. They had the ability to see the souls, the "neshamas", of their followers, and thus be able to diagnose their weaknesses and needs for spiritual growth.

The synagogues and temples that now exist are just sort of temporary functioning places for worship. They are not replacements for and don't function as The Temple. In fact, the Orthodox maintain that no place of worship in Judaism should be called a "temple". Reform Judaism took on the word "temple" for their houses of worship because they wanted to distinguish themselves from the Orthodox. But the Orthodox believe there is only one Temple, and that is the one that existed in Jerusalem and is supposed to exist again. Nothing else should be called a "temple" or "*the* temple". They're called "synagogues" by the Orthodox, which is actually a Greek word, or "schul", which is a Yiddish word.

Rabbis are regarded as just learned, dedicated religious leaders, although the term also means "master". There are different rabbinical schools where you can get a degree and you're officially a rabbi. Traditionally, one rabbi could train and ordain another as a rabbi. Although it has lost emphasis in recent times, in the old country (pre-industrial revolution Europe), there were rabbinic lineages within Judaism. There is still an emphasis in yoga concerning lineages, partly because it establishes a basis for genuine authority. Hasidism has retained a similar type of emphasis on lineage, tracing lines back to its originator, the Baal Shem Tov. But since the destruction of the Second Temple, there is no High Priest and there are no kind of functions or sacraments as conducted when the Temple existed.

The Messiah and The Third Temple

So what about the coming of the Messiah and the rebuilding of the Temple, the establishment of the Third Temple? One conception of Messiah is that Messiah in and of him/her/itself cannot do a thing until everyone is ready for that function to activate. If we are not receptive to the Messiah function, the Messiah can't do anything of its own accord except to be. In a way, Messiah is waiting. It's not like Messiah is "coming", rather, Messiah is "waiting". Messiah is waiting until we're ready to make use of Messiah. If rebuilding the Temple is part of that, first there has to be the groundwork for it to be done in the right way, or it won't happen, just as Messiah won't happen. A lot of people, including many Orthodox Jews, think the Messiah is overdue. Why hasn't Messiah come? Because the Messiah isn't going to go around bopping people on the head and showing them the light. We already have to see a lot of the light. If we don't, we wouldn't recognize the Messiah from a hole in the wall, or utilize Messiah for what Messiah is supposed to be utilized. It is similar to the conception, "when the student is ready, the teacher will appear", but on a collective level. When society is ready, the Messiah will appear. There is always opportunity to advance on an individual level. But there also is a group level, a collective level, and there has to be enough advancement on a group level for Messiah to function, for the Third Temple to appear.

Some conceptions of the Messiah change. Jesus lived during the time of the Second Temple. Obviously, there was already the idea of the Messiah at that time, which couldn't have included the building of the Third Temple, as the Second Temple still existed. Yet, there was a conception of a Savior to come from the

House of David to rescue the world from its iniquities. Many Jews at the time of Jesus and after his death claimed Jesus was the Messiah. They didn't see themselves as Christians; that distinction came later. They were a segment of Judaism that accepted Jesus as the Messiah. Eventually, through the processes of the next few hundred years, they stopped regarding themselves as Jewish and started calling themselves Christians. The ones who did not accept Jesus as the Messiah remained identified as Jews. For them, Jesus wasn't the Messiah because he didn't fit their definition. Did Jesus have an impact, both spiritual and otherwise? There seems to be no question, especially concerning what has been done in his name by people who thereafter have called themselves Christians. Who knows what the world would be like if Jesus didn't come. But now, Christians are waiting for the Second Coming, while Jews are still waiting for the First Coming. And Buddhists are awaiting Maitreya, and Hindus are awaiting Kalki. And so it goes.

In current Jewish Orthodoxy and Hasidism, there is more and more talk about the Messiah coming soon. The Messiah is around the corner. There is great hope in the Messiah coming. But the Messiah has been coming for centuries. There have been historic messianic movements in Judaism in addition to the multitude of such movements in Christianity. There have been false messiahs that have come, who have garnered the support of many important authorities of the day, only to fall by the wayside. One of them, in the 1600's, Sabbatai Zvi, was offered the choice to be beheaded or convert to Islam. He chose to convert and that was the end of that. He was the biggest one, and it was a great embarrassment to the Jewish establishment. Another earlier one was Simon bar Kochba, a para-military figure leading rebellions against the Romans in the second century CE, known for his ferociousness and designated as the Messiah by Rabbi Akiva, a well-respected scholar and authority both in his day and throughout the centuries, even to the current time. Bar Kochba and Akiva were both killed by the Romans. There have been many other messianic movements throughout the centuries claiming that the Messiah is either here or right around the corner. We are at one of those junctures again, especially emphasized in Jewish quarters by the Orthodox and the Hasidim, in addition to Christian denominations claiming the imminent Second Coming of Christ.

Yoga and mysticism have taught that assistance is always available. There are always entities ready to help. If we don't turn to use the help, if we don't avail ourselves of them, they are limited in what they can do to help us. That's why Jesus has to come again. That's why Buddha has to come again. And the Jews are still waiting for the Messiah the first time! Jesus didn't fit their definition. Their definition on a literal level is that there has to be a physical reestablishment of the

Temple, people who have been dead in the grave for the last three thousand years are physically going to come out of the grave, regenerate their bodies and start living again. These are some of the Jewish ideas of what's going to happen when the real deal comes, and that's why they reject Jesus as the Messiah. People didn't emerge from their graves and reconstitute flesh back onto their skeletons and start functioning again. That's one reason. Now talk about figurative versus literal! There are people who pay a lot of money for a gravesite in a particular cemetery in the Jerusalem area because they think if they're buried there, they're going to be the first ones to come up! There's that whole "first" thing again. Who's going to be first? What is the advantage to being first?

The whole conception of the dead literally, physically being raised is locked into a certain model in this physical realm. A more mystical and yogic interpretation of that takes into account reincarnation, which has always been prevalent in yogic thought, but also has a basis in Jewish mysticism, although traditional mainstream Jewish thought does not subscribe to it. Those beings who died without full realization will continue to have opportunities to experience a more full realization in subsequent reincarnations. During their incarnations coinciding with the appearance of the Messiah, the power of the presence of the Messiah will elevate those beings into a new realm of life. In that sense, it is similar to the Christian sense of being reborn. Those same entities who died many past physical deaths are going to have an opportunity to experience a new revelation accompanied by a new level of vibrational existence. This conception of raising of the dead is more conceivable and less far-fetched than the traditional idea of a physical, bodily process occurring.

A similar view can be taken concerning the rebuilding of the Temple, the appearance of the Third Temple. Maybe the Temple is not supposed to exist in the physical realm as we now know it. Maybe it is supposed to exist in some other realm. The traditional Jewish viewpoint is that the physical realm is the endpoint of all of creation and it is therefore very important for things to occur on the physical realm. That's what we're about. But a different approach from a mystical point of view is that life is all about evolution. What we now perceive as the physical mode may literally be dropping off, and we may be entering into a higher realm of vibrational existence which, if and when we get there, may seem similar to what we now consider the physical realm, but there will be qualitative differences in that realm. So when you begin to examine what is real and what is physical and what is the endpoint and culmination of creation, you find that it is in flux. This worldly existence is either going to elevate up to a higher vibrational level or drop off if it can't make the transition. If it elevates to a higher vibrational level, what becomes the endpoint will have a different qualitative nature to it than what is now the endpoint. From that point of view, some interpretations of the traditional Jewish concepts take on a different slant.

Is the Third Temple really going to physically appear, as Orthodox Jews believe, on the physical level as we now know it? Are they going to conduct the sacrifices again, the physical slaughtering of the animals and all the rituals, just like they did over 2000 years ago? It is hard to accept that this is what is supposed to occur. There is a notion that the Temple is a reflection of a Heavenly Temple, in accord with the dual conceptions that we are to bring heaven down to earth, while at the same time, elevating earth to heaven. The Temple is also seen as being symbolic of the human body. Additionally, as has previously been discussed in Chapter One, in addition to this heaven-to-earth vertical exchange, there is also an earth-to-earth lateral interchange, with the Temple facing East, to receive the energy generated there and then retransmit it to the West, functioning as this giant receiver/transmitter. With these models in mind, it seems that after all of this time, we are supposed to be shifting to a higher and more subtle level of functioning, consistent with the conception of a paradigm shift, and that this new Temple will exist at a different vibratory level. Possibly, its construction may have already commenced at that level. What had been acted out on the gross external plane in the past would be acted out on a more subtle, more internalized level from the start. There may not need to be physical attendance at a physical location as we now conceive of it, as these events would all occur on a more transcendental level. A collective consciousness could create this Third Temple on a more ethereal plane, and the individual sacrifices of our internal lower animal natures could be taken to and consumed at that altar, the process of this transmutation setting forth a pleasing aroma, all at a transcendental level of functioning. Consider it. A new age of gentleness would not require the kinds of gross physicality as in the past. It might be real on some level, but not on levels that are now commonly conceived. Perhaps we need to at least consider other possibilities.

Chapter Four

The Cosmic Egg and the Tree of Life
The Mind and Emotions
Tradition and Reformation
Study, Study, Study

The Cosmic Egg and The Tree of Life

Swami Rama passed away in 1996. In the period after he passed away, it appears that many of his students endured various types of inner agitation and shifting, both positive and negative. There was a lot of turmoil at the Institute [The Himalayan Institute of Yoga Science and Philosophy, headquartered in Honesdale, PA, founded by Swami Rama], which I, thankfully, wasn't directly exposed to because I wasn't there. Unless you have had a relationship with a being like this, it is hard to describe what that relationship fully entailed. I personally shy away from the term "guru". For me, he was my spiritual mentor, my spiritual father, and that is the terminology he once used, that he was my spiritual father. The funny thing is that in retrospect, I realized that I had a dream revelation a month earlier providing me with a "heads up" that he was about to pass away, but I didn't interpret the message properly at the time, so it was still a real surprise and shock when I was informed. The way I heard about it was they sent out letters to everybody. I received this letter in the mail, and without even opening it, I could see what it said. My immediate response was that I started to cry like a baby. I was just bawling my eyes out. After I got over that, my next reaction was, "my loss, his gain". In the weeks and months that followed, I had an image that when he died, it was like a fireworks exploding in the inner spiritual sky. When this fireworks exploded in the inner spiritual sky, it created all of these sparks. There is an interesting connection, as you may recall my discussion earlier in this book about Divine Sparks in Jewish mysticism. These sparks, like fireworks, descended to earth and fell on some of his students who were fortunate enough to be at the right time and place to receive them. I felt like one of these sparks hit me, as others hit other students. After it hit me, that spark caused an explosion within which resulted in a creative, revelatory surge. I think it was one way in which he passed his mantle on to his students.

One image that emerged from the gestation of that spark being implanted in me was of a glyph that has correspondences to the Kabalistic Tree of Life, although this was before I started studying Kabala. That image generated certain conceptions which were encapsulated within it. I have labeled that image the "Cosmic Egg" [see figure 1 at the end of this chapter]. If you are familiar with depictions of the Tree of Life [see figures 2 and 3 at the end of this chapter], you can see how it corresponds to the top part of the Tree of Life depicting the first three Sephirot of Kether, Chokmah and Binah, and the three rings above Kether (traditionally depicted as in figure 3), depicted in the Cosmic Egg figure as three circles aligned vertically, one above another, with everything enclosed in an egg-shaped circumference. In Kabala, the three rings beyond Kether are sometimes illustrated as being interlaced, but others depict one above the other. In the Cosmic Egg depiction that came to me, within the Cosmic Egg are the levels beyond manifestation. The highest level is what in the Yoga tradition is referred to as "Brahman". My revelation was that pure spirit is a very subtle, slight separation from this unfathomable Brahman from which everything arises, indicated by the second highest level. And then at the third level, the first force that isn't even force in the way that we commonly conceive of it, but is the real initiating essence that leads to separation, polarity, is pure love/grace/intent/will. So what conceptually came to me first graphically, in what I would call a pre-intellectual mode, followed by an intellectualization, was this image depicting a subtle process whereby Pure Spirit/Consciousness arises out of Brahman, and Pure Divine Love, relating to Grace, Will and Intent emerges from Pure Spirit, and proceeds in a subtle fashion to simultaneously proceed down the middle, and also separate into the first side polarities. The most basic polarity is Divine Light and Divine Sound. Light is on the right side of Force, and Sound is on the left side of Form. There is the symbol of Infinity connecting these two, depicting that an infinite combination of the vibrations and energies of Light and Sound create everything else. The realm of Absolute Unmanifest potentiality exists prior to the polarization, and the realm of relativity, manifest actuality, begins with the first polarity. So this image came to me before I started studying Kabala, and as can be seen by its similarities to the Tree of Life figures, it was obviously a precursor, a preconditioning for my study of Kabala. Not too long after I had this revelation, I was led to the Karin Kabalah Center to help fill in the gaps and complete the picture. My focus had generally been more on the ultimate, the unmanifest, which is why I think my revelation only went so far. But to more capably function in this world, it is helpful to fill in the gaps with more detail.

In all of the yogic scriptures that I've seen and all of the descriptions that I've read, there are numerous references to Divine Light and Divine Sound. Certainly at some level, light and sound are very different. Of course, tracing them back to their source, they ultimately have a common origin; light and sound eventually become one in Cosmic Divine Fire. There they merge, but when they separate, light is more associated with force and sound is what gives rise to form. You can almost feel the physicality of the vibrations emanating from sound. Of course you can feel the heat of the light of the sun, but as our science informs us, it is of a different quality and nature, more aligned with force. So my revelation depicted this interplay of light on the right/force side and sound on the left/form side.

It is the interplay of light and sound, of force and form, that creates everything else. Swami Rama often described this as a process of descending down through "degrees and grades". Kabala refers to it as the process of "involution", moving through the worlds from the most subtle to the most gross. It involves down through various degrees and grades. I came to realize that Swami Rama was referring to this same process detailed in the Tree of Life, without going into a lot of specifics. And he often used the terminology, "degrees and grades". He led me to come to the Karin Kabalah Center to figure that out and fill in the details, the gaps. And after that, through my continuing study of Jewish sources, I found that the Zohar, one of the significant texts of Jewish mysticism, uses the exact same terminology describing the same process: "degrees and grades".

I am quite certain that Swami Rama was behind the revelation provided to me of the Cosmic Egg, and that he provided the impetus that led me to the Karin Kabalah Center. Another gap-filler was a subsequent revelation that the unified "substance", if you want to call it that, encompassing both Divine Light and Divine Sound simultaneously in one form, from which the first polarity emerges, is Divine Fire, called "Agni" in yoga. Internal and external fire have correspondences. They both emit light and sound. And thus, as discussed in Chapter One, the Roerichs coined the term, "Agni Yoga".

The Mind and Emotions

Please bear in mind that what I'm doing here is presenting Judaism through the eyes of a yogi. As stated elsewhere, my background has been in the study and practice of yoga. However, I've been led to explore Judaism, but I'm seeing it through the eyes of yoga. It is important, therefore, to present some of the yoga contexts through which I am operating. From there, we can move into the connections I have discovered between yoga and Judaism. There is a basic yogic description of the mind and its functions. Swami Rama would say that the physical body is our "external instrument", our external tool; the mind is our "internal instrument", our internal tool. We are not our minds, just as we are not our bodies. The mind is a tool and an instrument for us to utilize. Our inner spirit utilizes the mind just as the mind utilizes the body. It is helpful to compare the yoga designations for parts and functions of the mind to the operation of a computer. It is interesting to analogize the mind to a computer, because it seems like the structure for the artificial intelligence we have created is comparable to the structure of our nature-imbued intelligence.

There is what is called the vast storehouse of the mind. It includes all of the parts of the mind, the functions of the mind, and is also the repository for our memories, images and experience. It is called the "citta", and it is comparable to the hard drive on a computer. Next is the part of the mind generally referred to as the "lower mind", which takes care of all of our autonomic functioning, involuntary systems, lower level processing, storage and retrieval of information, which is called "manas", from which is derived the words "man" and "mind". It is comparable to the RAM, software and operating system in a computer. It is there and automatically taking care of certain functions, ready for manipulation by the computer operator. When the computer is turned on, the electricity, which is akin to the basic life force called "prana" in yoga, begins flowing, the RAM and operating system kick in, and certain software loads, ready to go. When the computer is turned off, which is akin to dying, these systems cease their stand-by functioning; the mind as we generally think of it, is basically gone. The potentialities for all of these operations revert back to the hard drive. They are still there, but they're not functioning as they would be if the computer was turned on and electricity, prana, was flowing. The "ahamkara" in yogic literature is basically the ego, a sense of self separate from everything else. It is akin to the computer operator sitting at the computer eager to do something, because the ego likes activity, especially self-reinforcing activity. Then there is the higher mind or intellect, the "buddhi", which is the operator actually beginning to do something, to serve his or her purposes. It is the source for our discrimination, our discernment, our higher intelligence. Our lower intelligence takes care of the automatic pilot and standby functions satisfactorily. But when we need to make choices, decide on courses of action, discriminate, distinguish, we use our buddhi, our higher intelligence. That's the basic yogic layout of how the mind works and functions.

What are emotions? Where do they come from? What are their source? Why are they there? What am I supposed to do with them? For many years I struggled with those questions. I repeatedly heard lectures that were providing the answers, but I wasn't getting it. Finally, somewhere along the line, a light came on. Swami Rama would frequently talk in his lectures about the "primitive fountains of life" or the "cities of life". The primitive fountains of life are basically our animal instincts, which are the source of our lower emotional levels. He identified these four: food, sex, sleep and self-preservation. He emphasized our need to control and direct them, and not be controlled by them. Through analyzing these more closely, I came to the observation that food, sex and sleep seem to be sub-divisions of self-preservation, which seems to be the most primal of all. Food and sleep are needed for self-preservation, and sex provides for procreation, which is a form of self-preservation. Sex doesn't mean just sex in a narrow sense, but includes all sensate, sensual activities: the seeking out of pleasure and the avoidance of pain, pursuits which are secondary to self-preservation. These are addressing a basic level of survival instincts: fight or flight, preserve your life at all costs. There is a natural urge, a natural drive to do what is necessary to survive. What he has said is that all of our emotions are tied to one of these basic primal instincts. And it seems to me that most emotions can be referred back to self-preservation; maybe not all, but most. A major motivation and concern is security. Self-preservation and the drive to survive relates to our need to feel secure and our discomfort at feeling insecure, whether such a threat is real or only perceived. Many TV preachers appeal to their audience's emotion-based sense of wanting to feel safe, secure, comfortable and certain that there is this trustworthy higher being that is looking after them. A lot of our actions are dictated by these urges, these instincts. In Jewish thought, they would be referred to as the lower animal urges, the lower animal instincts.

Well, being human is more than that. There is a higher level of emotion, a higher instinct, drive, urge. In the word "human", "hu" signifies the Divine, and "man" derives from a word meaning "mind"; "Hu-mans" are "Divine Minds". There is a higher level of emotion that originates in the Spiritual Heart. This higher level of emotion yearns to experience and express Divinity, to connect with our inner Spirit and celebrate what it finds. Sometimes the lower and higher emotions are in conflict. Added to this mix is the mind and the ego. The ego and emotions often consort, resulting in the mind being engaged in pursuits to preserve the ego, the sense of separation. The ego does not want to die, be obliterated, or even become subservient to anything else, and it perceives many threats to its existence, both real and imagined. The ego wants to bolster itself, but by doing so, it heightens its sense of separation. The higher mind is responsible for seeing to it that the ego can still survive and function, but for purposes of aiding the higher emotional and intellectual level of functioning, not for its own self-aggrandizement. The ego needs to know its proper place; it does not need to be destroyed. There is a strain in yogic literature advancing the idea that the function of spiritual discipline is to destroy the ego; that the ego needs to be annihilated in order to attain liberation. This is somewhat exaggerated and misleading. A more correct approach is that the ego doesn't have to be annihilated, but it needs to know its place. When the ego is running the show and uses the higher intellect as its servant, fueled and driven by the lower emotions and instincts, that's when we get out of kilter. When the instincts and inspiration of the higher level of the Spirit utilize the higher intellect to direct our lives and place things in their proper perspective, then the higher intellect can also put the ego to its proper use: as a servant to the higher instincts and work with the higher mind to skillfully, selflessly and lovingly perform our duties and actions in the world.

I initially had difficulty relating with the frequent references in the Torah and commentaries about emotion and heart in a negative sense. In my studies of yoga and Eastern mysticism, there were frequent references to the heart in a positive sense. This was in respect to the higher aspect of heart, that the Heart as the seat of inner Divine Love needs to be running the show. Even higher intellect should be subservient to Heart, as the Heart is the source of the highest wisdom, not the intellect. I kept a fortune from a special fortune cookie that says "the Heart is wiser than the intellect". Well, in Torah commentary, there are many teachings about the heart having to be controlled by the mind because they're talking about the lower heart comprising the lower animal instincts. When we talk about athletes having a lot of heart, what are we referring to? They'll fight to the bitter end until they're laying on the floor unconscious and can't go on. They find incredible reserves of strength. They're boxing or they're playing basketball as if their life depended on it; it is at the lower level of heart related to self-preservation. Not all athletes can do that, but some athletes are known and admired for the depth of their heart. But that all relates to the heart at the lower level, not at the higher level. Many of the Torah commentaries maintain that the heart at this level has to be controlled. Perhaps it is acceptable on the sporting fields, but in the larger arena of life, you can't let the lower primitive instincts, drives, urges run wild; you have to control them with the will-power of the higher intellect. So Jewish teachings tend to focus on self-control through utilization of the higher mind. Certain paths of yoga also emphasize this process, viewing the higher intellect as the source and tool for will-power and self-discipline. But ultimately, the higher emotion, the Heart, the source of Divine Love should be the prime motivator controlling and directing the higher and lower minds, the ego and the lower emotions. There are some references in the Torah and the Jewish commentaries about this higher emotional Divine level of heart. But you don't find it discussed as much as the idea of study, study, study; use your intelligence, your higher discriminatory intellect coupled with your will-power to control the lower urges, to sublimate them. This is balanced by abundant use of emotion-based spiritual practices of prayer and observances of acknowledgement and praise of the Divine Being, intended to sublimate the lower urges, keeping them in their proper perspective, and not letting them rule your life. Prayer is a powerful aid, connecting with the higher emotional level, invoking the higher Heart. You just don't find an emphasis on operating through the Heart in the conduct of daily activity discussed or encouraged very often in the Jewish sources.

Although circumcision is usually related to circumcising the male sex organ, there is an interesting reference in the Torah concerning circumcision of the heart. The idea behind circumcising the male sex organ is to release the lower instinctual sexual energy to help transform it and sublimate it to a higher energy. The same goes with the heart in this reference to circumcision of the heart. The idea is that just as with the male sex organ, the heart also has a membrane, a layer over it that is restricting it from actualizing its full potential. If the heart is circumcised, then the higher level of heart can be expressed. That is obviously figurative and not literal!

Tradition and Reformation

There's an old joke that addresses some themes and issues concerning spirituality, religion, belief and tradition. There is a well-known secular version, but this is a lesser-known Jewish version. As part of their training, rabbinic students get sent out to various temples and synagogues to observe the different ways that religious services are conducted. In Judaism, there are variations among the different branches, and there are even variations within the same branch. This assignment is designed to give the rabbinic students a feel as to how things are done and expose them to the differences among congregations as how the different prayers and ceremonies are performed. A particular rabbinic student had attended and observed many services in different congregations. Along the way, he was taking notes about the variations. On this one occasion, he came across a wrinkle that was quite peculiar; he hadn't seen anything like it anywhere else, so it piqued his interest. In Judaism, during the conduct of prayers, there is what is called "davenning". Particularly in Orthodox practice, davenning involves a lot of swaying of the body. There is a bending of the knees and bowing forward, which is the Jewish equivalent of kneeling, but there is no actual kneeling on the knees. There's standing, there's sitting, and there's one particular series of prayers performed entirely standing up. So there are these various bodily motions, all of which were familiar to the rabbinic student. Now, the pulpit in Judaism is called the "bimah", which is generally an area like a church pulpit, a raised platform from which the services are conducted and where the Ark containing the Torah scroll is kept. There are usually steps up to it, at the front or on the sides, for access to it by members in the congregation who are called up to the bimah at various times during the service. Well, in this congregation, whenever anyone would go up to the bimah, there would be some place along the way where they would do this kind of motion, a movement with the torso of the body, first leaning to one side, then leaning forward and stepping forward, then straightening back up again. When they exited the bimah, they'd do it again on the way down.

This student had had never seen anything like this. So after the service was concluded, he was talking with some of the congregants and asked them about it: "I've observed services in many congregations. I've seen several variations, but I've never seen anything like this movement that you do when you step onto and off of the bimah. What is the significance behind this movement?" They all started scratching their heads and responded, "We really don't know. We've always done it here at this congregation. It's just something we've always done." No-one seemed to remember why, and they weren't even aware that it was so unusual. So they're pondering this when something starts to come back to an older fellow. He says, "You know, I think I remember now. I think I recall where this comes from. You see, years ago, we started out in the basement of a church before we got this building of our own. Where we had the bimah, there was a low-hanging pipe overhead, and whenever anyone had to go up to the bimah, they had to get out of the way of the pipe!" The secular version of this joke conveys the same message, but it has to do with a similarly obsolete method of cooking roast beef.

The main point behind this joke is to illustrate a situation where these people were mindlessly doing this ritual without having any idea as to its significance. Not only was it devoid of any significant ritual meaning, it had outlived its original purpose which no-one remembered anyway. So on one level, they were doing something as mindless habit. That's the critical view and message to the story. They're doing something, they don't even know why they're doing it, and it just solidified and crystallized into this mindless, almost superstitious, practice. Maybe it's time to look at it anew and reconsider its purpose and usefulness. But then from another point of view, okay, now they know why they are doing it; someone has remembered. Maybe they should keep doing it just to honor the humble beginnings of the congregation, as a gesture, a reminder of where they came from, and maybe it's okay to keep it. But at least they know why; before they didn't know why. And then, yet another level would be, let it go. It's obsolete. It's outlived its purpose. It's time to move on. So this little joke illustrates an issue that many religious traditions struggle with about dogma, doctrine, ritual, liturgy and all of that. It embodies issues that have led to reform movements and the creation of new denominations in many religions. How much do you hold on to, how much do you let go? Is there room for anything new, for adaptation to changing times and circumstances? In most religious traditions, there is sort of a cutoff point; the canon has been closed, this is decided, this is our sacred literature. Nothing can be added to it or subtracted from it after this point; our liturgy is closed, our ritual is closed. Whatever certain authorities determined, that is as far as we're going to go. You can't add, subtract or revise anything. The question is, why not? It is an ongoing issue struggled with by most traditions. It remains a major struggle within Judaism.

When do you let go of certain old ways? Is there room for new ways? Where does the authority come from, where does the authentication come from for the new ways? Who do you trust to ascertain whether something is genuine or not? Many traditions, many spiritual teachers look for authentication in some manner. That's why there is so much pounding of the Bible. "It's in the Bible". They want it authenticated, they want it verified, they want certainty. "This is not just coming from me, the Bible says it". Well, at what point do you go beyond that? That is a theme, a far-ranging issue. It has always been an issue in Judaism and it still is today, about balancing all of these considerations, letting go of some of the old that doesn't seem relevant anymore. How do you infuse new and still have a spirit there? One of the problems is that sometimes the reformers remove the spirit. I am not a regular in synagogue attendance; I go once in a blue moon, and usually out of some obligation, for a wedding or Bar/Bat Mitzvah. But if I wanted to go and had my choice, I would still rather go to an Orthodox synagogue, because to me there is more spirit, or as my childhood rabbi put it, there is more real "communion with God" going on in an Orthodox synagogue than I usually have seen in a Reform temple. What I generally have experienced in Reform temples is starchiness, with the service presented more as a performance and the congregation regarded more as an audience, rather than as participants. I've seen only glimmers here and there of real spirit. Of course, the Reform can counter that the Orthodox practices are too arcane and inaccessible to many people, and thus the impetus for reform movements.

One last thought about following or breaking rules: sometimes there will be some highly elevated being who breaks almost every rule in the book when performing traditional ceremonies. There are the rules, like the Brahmins in India might perform in their rigid ritualistic way, and then you hear of a God-infused being, like a Ramakrishna, who performs the rituals, but breaks many of the rules along the way. Rules become secondary for the God-intoxicated. Such a being is infused with spirit, and maybe he does or maybe he doesn't follow the rules. I once was watching an old new age movie called "Sunseed" with a friend who is a professor of Sufism at the University of Georgia. One focus in the movie centers around a personage known as Sufi Sam, Samuel Lewis, who was quite a character. My professor friend noted that Sufi Sam was mangling the pronunciation of certain prayers that he was intoning. But because it was Sufi Sam, it didn't matter because he was obviously infused with spirit. It came out the way it came out. So be it!

Study, Study, Study

The Jewish tradition has always emphasized study, study, study. You've got to study Torah, study Talmud, study this, study that; and there are volumes of stuff to study. Studying is done both alone and with groups reading and debating and discussing, taking every single word and subject and inspecting them all, looking at them in every conceivable way, including ways that most people would hardly dream of, reading all of these meanings into every single thing. There are numerological and phonectic aspects, searching for the significance behind names, words or phrases that have the same numerical value, sound the same, look the same, or are even close, although not exactly the same, in some respect or other. The extent of the analyses, interpretations and extrapolations is remarkable. There has been some valid criticism that it can get too preposterous or too dry and intellectual and become an exercise in mental gymnastics devoid of any real spiritual significance. But there nevertheless can be deeper dimensions and benefits to the study. Group study fosters relationships and community, and whether in a group or alone, an inner transformative effect can occur through the study.

Any good spiritual program, like the one at the Karin Kabalah Center, is more than an intellectual academic exercise. As the Karin course is described, it involves a "process of transformation". The process of self-study of Torah and Jewish sources that I have undertaken has been similar. There is an intellectual, academic level, in which I'm sitting down with these texts and poring over these books and materials, reading the commentaries, comparing translations and commentaries, going on the Internet to glean even more information. But at the same time, there is definitely an internal experiential level that is taking place while my mind and body is engaged in that process. There is an inner transformative process that happens at the same time. One can imagine that the scholars and sages throughout the ages who have dedicated themselves to Torah study, at least some of them some of the time, were also undergoing more than just an intellectual exercise. I don't think I could keep doing it if I wasn't sensing the transformative effects, because otherwise, it would become insufferably tedious. It can get pretty tedious anyway.

Despite the emphasis on study and the intellectual side, Judaism has also always employed prayer as a balance to all of the studying. In traditional Judaism, you pray three times a day. Prayer is a physical and emotional counterbalance, providing a break for the mind. It is important in most Jewish prayer practices that you don't do it alone; you do it with other people, again emphasizing community and collective effort. Other common activities in traditional Jewish communities that moderate the tedium and intensity of all of the studying include robust singing and dancing, often augmented by more than a touch of alcohol!

FIGURE 1 – THE COSMIC EGG

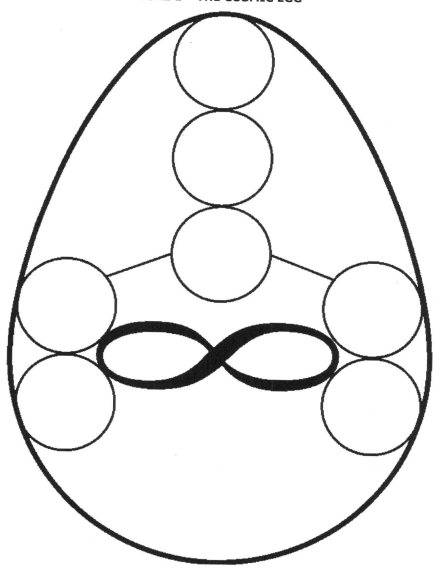

FIGURE 2 – THE TREE OF LIFE, LURIANIC VERSION

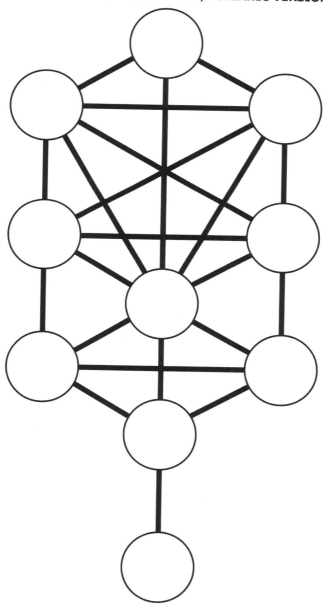

FIGURE 3 – THE TREE OF LIFE, KARIN VERSION, WITH THE THREE RINGS

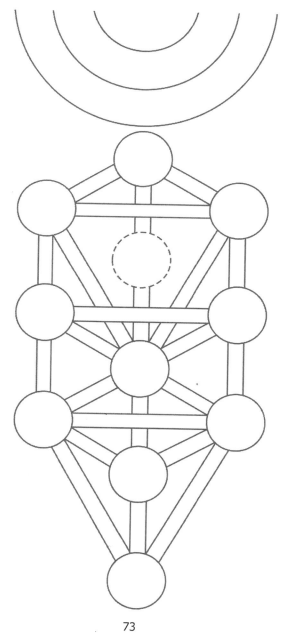

Chapter Five

Positive Aspects to Darkness
The Mechanics of Creation
The Serpent Power

Positive Aspects to Darkness

In many mystical traditions, there is a focus on Light. Darkness is seen as a bad and evil thing and the embodiment of ignorance. Wherever there is light, there cannot be darkness. Light dispels darkness. Light dispels ignorance. Although acknowledging that aspect, I have always felt that darkness gets a bad rap, because there is an additional positive aspect to darkness that gets overlooked. There is a place for darkness; it is not just ignorance and the absence of light. We're born in wombs; we benefit from the nurturance found in that darkness. When we meditate, we generally turn off the lights; maybe we have a candle, maybe we don't. We utilize dimmed light in our external environment to assist our entry into a dark, womb-like place within, even in our search for inner light. Mystical Judaism contains a rarely found viewpoint about this positive aspect to darkness. There is a type of darkness described that is not just the absence of light; darkness is a substance in and of itself. There are references to a "lamp of darkness", this paradoxical lamp that generates darkness instead of light. The Torah recites that one of the plagues in Egypt was the plague of darkness. That darkness was not just the absence of light, it was an aspect of this positive substance of darkness. It was so dark, you couldn't see your hand in front of your face. So there is a place for darkness, not only as a symbol of evil or ignorance, but also as a certain nurturing medium that we need in addition to light. Jewish sources even categorize three types of darkness: the one in the plague in Egypt, the one in the pillar/cloud that accompanied/led the Hebrews during the day in their wanderings after the Exodus, and the darkness that descended upon Mt. Sinai when God directly addressed the multitude after the Exodus.

The Mechanics of Creation

An important perspective and framework for a discussion about the creation process is succinctly summarized in the title of a wonderful book on Jewish mysticism: *God Is a Verb*, by Rabbi David Cooper. Implicit in this discussion is the idea that creation as described in Genesis is not something that only happened in the mythic past, whether literal or figurative. "Genesis" – beginning, creating, sustaining – is happening all of the time and at all levels, from cosmic to individual. That is why such a detailed discussion of it is relevant, because it includes a description of an ongoing process occurring everywhere and within everything at all levels all of the time. Perhaps most importantly, it provides a blueprint for a deeper inner understanding of one's Self. Remember: all that is without is within, and vice versa.

Let us begin by expanding upon an earlier discussion in this book concerning what is being conveyed in the glyphs of the Cosmic Egg (Figure 1 at the end of Chapter 4) and the Tree of Life (Figure 3 at the end of Chapter 4). There appear to be three aspects that are at the foundation of mystical experience existing within the realm of the unmanifest beyond the worlds. There is a designation in the Vedic tradition of something called "Brahman". This realm is beyond description; it can only be referred to. In quantum physics, there is something called the "unified field", and it would appear that Brahman is its ancient Vedic correlate. It is this unified field from which everything emanates. Mysteriously inter-related with Brahman, or arising out of this indefinable field, is "pure spirit" – unadulterated spirit in its purest form, which is basically synonymous with "pure awareness," "pure consciousness." And then, mysteriously emanating out of that, but still within the realm of the unmanifest field, is pure Divine Love. The universe emanates out of this Love, and is sustained and embraced by it. God is Love. All of this exists in a realm beyond what we generally conceive of as energy – beyond force, beyond form. However, something exists there that is sort of like a force, but I wouldn't call it a force. And there is something that you could say is like a power – we talk about the "power of love" – but it is not power in the same way that we conceive of force or energy as being a power. There is the power of Divine Love, the power of Divine Spirit, of unadulterated pure consciousness, pure awareness, which permeates existence, permeates the manifest world, but is paradoxically beyond at the same time. It travels down the middle pillar of the Tree of Life to the lowest level of the lowest world, but it originates in, and simultaneously remains in, a realm beyond the highest level of the highest world. It is both the source of existence and the underlying medium through which existence functions.

In the Vedic/yoga tradition, there is something designated as "Sat Chit Ananda", "Being, Consciousness, Bliss". That is a similar trinity describing this realm. "Sat" is generally translated as "Being", "Existence", and "Truth". Pure being in its most pure form is Truth, the foundation of existence, which can't be referred to other than saying it just is; it is "Isness" in its most pure form. "Chit" is that pure consciousness of spirit as described above. "Ananda", primordial bliss, includes Divine Love as described above. There is another word for love in yoga, "prem". But in addition to incorporating joy and bliss, "Ananda" is the term which designates that which proceeds out from the state of joy and bliss: the primordial impulse to emanate and sustain creation encompassed in Divine Love.

The related trinity in Kabala is "Ein", "Ein Soph", and "Ein Soph Or", corresponding to The Ring Cosmos, The Ring Chaos, and The Ring Pass Not respectively, as designated in Christian Kabala. There has been some confusion about the word "Ein" due to differing English transliterations and Hebrew pronunciations. Sometimes it is spelled "E-I-N", "Ein" and is pronounced like the "ain" in the word "paint". Other times, it is spelled "A-Y-I-N", and is pronounced "Ah-yin", which is the same pronunciation and spelling as one of the Hebrew letters.It is represented both ways by different sources, although referring to the same thing. Additional confusion, but perhaps also mystical insight, is created by the fact that the name for the letter "Ayin" is also a word which means "eye" and "well/spring/fountain". The Ein/Ayin of Kabala means "Not", "Nothing", "Nothingness" similar to Buddhist concepts of "Shunyata/The Void", and is spelled with the consonants Aleph, Yod and Nun. The word meaning "eye" contains the consonants Ayin, Yod and Nun, and is pronounced "ah-yin". The word meaning "well/spring" uses the same consonants as the word for eye, but different vowels producing the pronunciation of "ain" as in "paint", phonetically similar to the word meaning "Nothing". I say "phonetically similar" because although the consonants Aleph and Ayin today are often both regarded as silent letters, Ayin historically had a slight guttural sound, still intoned by some today, and the letter is still classified as a guttural in most Hebrew texts, unlike Aleph. Nevertheless, the phonetic similarity of these words appears to be more than mere coincidence. The saying about the eyes being the windows to the soul, the very essence of an individual found deep within, seems to be appropriately mirrored by the idea of wells being portals to the waters that sustain life on earth, just as the mysterious realm of "Ein" is designated by Kabala as the Ultimate Source of All. It is no coincidence that the Jewish Patriarchs were very involved with digging, maintaining, and re-digging wells, and that many key events in the Torah evolved around the setting of a well. There is the literal significance of the importance of a primary source of water in the scorched Middle East of Biblical times, often ravished by famine, but there appears to also be a deeper symbolic meaning.

In Hebrew, letters are also words and numbers, and the 22 letters of the Hebrew alphabet are also ascribed to the 22 paths on the Tree of Life (the paths being what connect the various spheres/Sephirot, providing avenues for the interaction of their energies). Yet another interesting aspect about the letter "Ayin" is that it is also a name for a path on the Tree, although there is disagreement among different Kabalists as to which letter goes with which path. There are meanings and significances to the energies associated with the paths. One scheme assigns "Ayin" to the path related to the devil. It is interesting to ponder that the window to the soul leads to the devil. Inner demons must be confronted and overcome on the path to the Source of everything, and everything includes the devil. All of our great mythical heroes have had to overcome adversity, conquer demons, and resist temptation.

Getting back to the realm beyond the world of the Trees, there is the Ein/Ayin, Nothingness (referred to hereafter only as "Ein"), "Ein Soph", referred to as "Everythingness", and "Ein Soph Or", the Nothingness and Everythingness infused with diffused Light. This general definition of "Ein" is similar to the Buddhist conception of the Void. It is Nothingness, as in the Zen conception of "No-thing." "Ein Soph" is Everything, "Everythingness". So there is the "Nothingness" and there is the "Everythingness", and then there is the Nothingness/Everythingness paradox infused with diffused (meaning "not concentrated") Light. "Or" (sometimes transliterated as "Aur") means "Light". "Ein Soph Or" is this paradoxical existence of Nothingness/Everythingness infused with diffused Light. There is this realm of diffused Light that is not concentrated; Light and Darkness are co-existing at the level of Ein Soph Or. This paradoxical co-existence is possible because, as discussed above, Darkness is not just the absence of Light; darkness is a positive substance. So these two positive substances co-exist, even though it would seem by their nature that they would cancel each other out. The diffused Light nevertheless co-exists with the Darkness. For a simple illustration, consider the sky at night. We know that many of the multitude of stars we see are more powerful and more bright than our own sun. But in the sky at night, they are little dots of light existing in a vast inky expanse of darkness. Despite the tremendous power of their light, they still appear as little pinpoints in this great vast darkness. The Ein Soph Or is the same idea on inner and outer mystical levels; there are little pinpoints of light diffused and existing within a vast darkness.

Now to relate all of this to the process of creation as narrated in Genesis. There is one common notion that all the acts of creation involve the "Ten Utterances", the times when the narrative relates, "And God said...", "Vayomer", in Hebrew (it is interesting to note that in this narration of the creation process, the Hebrew prefix "va" meaning "and" is always attached to the operative verb, suggesting an ongoing process). But it appears that there are three aspects to the creative function at work. One aspect is speaking/word/sound, as with the Ten Utterances. Another is spirit/wind/breath/Divine Presence that hovered/moved over the face of the deep and that later breathed life into the nostrils of man (and into all breathing creatures). It is interesting that the term used for this spirit/wind/breath/Divine Presence is "Ruach" in Hebrew, which is elsewhere designated in a scheme of gradations of spirit as a level of spirit just one above the lowest level. It is also interesting that this Ruach "hovered" or "moved" over the face of the deep, indicating some type of pre-creation Divine activity and interaction. And the third aspect of the creative function, which actually appears first in the text, is something unnamed that could be called Divine Will/Intent, as there appears to be this initiating impulse of creation that does not involve either sound or breath. It is evident in the first sentence, before any utterances or reference to breath, and again in the fourth sentence, at a very significant juncture, when God divides/separates between the light and darkness. In the first sentence this impulse is found associated with the verb for creating, "barah", and in the fourth sentence, with the verb for dividing/separating, "yavdel".

There has been much discussion about the sequence, or lack thereof, of the events as narrated in the opening of Genesis. One common idea is reflected in a translation that the first thing that happened, as stated in the opening sentence, is that God created the heaven and earth, the beginning of polarity: "In the beginning God created the heaven and earth." (The Kaplan translation favors this version, as does the Revised Standard and the King James versions, although Kaplan acknowledges other versions containing different implications, as discussed below). Before that was the Nothingness of the Ein described by Kabala, the realm of the Ring Cosmos. This initial act of creation adds Soph to the Ein; Everythingness is added to Nothingness, the Kabalistic conception of the Ein Soph, the realm of the Ring Chaos, as there is of yet no organization at this level; it is the unfettered energy of all conceivable manifestation in an unmanifested state. If that isn't Chaos, I don't know what is! Concerning the Ten Utterances, as noted above, there is no utterance recited in the first sentence; it does not say, "*God said*, 'Let there be a heaven and an earth'." This first movement of creation, initiating the very Beginnings/Bereshith/Genesis of Something/Everything from Nothing, is a product of the most basic Mystery of Divine Will/Intent. Breath/spirit/wind appears next, in the second sentence. Sound, the first utterance, does not occur until the third sentence, when God says as the first utterance, "Let there be light". From a mystical point of view, in some sense, this supports a view that Divine Sound exists prior to Divine Light, and that Light in fact is generated by or emerges out of Sound. Another interpretation would be that Sound and Light are co-equals emerging simultaneously out of the Silence, co-existing in the realm of primordial fire, as fire emanates both sound and light, and the first sound is accompanied by the first light. In any case, this is consistent with the Vedic notion that all creation emanated out of the primordial sound and mother of all mantras, OM, the sound of Agni/Fire/Light.

Following the Genesis narrative chronologically, we see that darkness existed prior to light, and that when light was first created, it was somehow injected into the darkness without dispelling it. As described above, they somehow mysteriously, paradoxically co-existed in an undifferentiated state until God then separated/divided them. This corresponds with the Kabalistic conception of the Ein Soph Or, the Everythingness and Nothingness infused with diffused light, the realm of the Ring Pass Not. No separative entity can enter this realm and survive as a separate entity. No one can survive seeing God face to face.

There are many interesting aspects concerning this first activity of creation of heaven and earth. The second sentence describes the earth that has just been created as being without form and empty, except for "the face of the deep", suggesting water having depth and a surface. It is interesting to note that in the first sentence, the word used for heaven is "shamayim" while in the second sentence, there is reference only to "mayim", or water, being part of the earth. "Shamayim" is a combination of "eish", fire, and "mayim", water. (Eish/fire is also found in one of the words designating humans, "ish" for "man" and "isha" for "woman". As is later narrated in the text, man is also formed from the dust of the ground, "adamah", from which comes the name for Adam, with a root meaning "red blood". Thus, man appears to be a combination of fire and earth, into which is breathed the breath of life/the spirit of God). So there is this initial differentiation between earth (which appears to be a mixture of earth, "eretz" and water, "mayim") as distinguished from heaven, a mixture of primordial fire and water, with water as a common ingredient.

The second day's activities are also quite mystifying. Through an utterance, a sky/firmament is created, separating and distinguishing waters above and below it. This sky/firmament that divides the upper and lower waters, both called "mayim" is now on the second day designated as "shamayim", the same designation for what is translated in the first sentence on the first day as the "heaven" comprised of fire and water. So a substance composed of fire and water is serving as a dividing barrier between water above and water below.

An alternative translation/interpretation of the first sentence, noted by Kaplan as advanced by some commentators and reflected in the Stone/Artscroll translation, is "In the beginning of God's creation of heaven and earth, the earth (or when the earth...)". These translations, either implying the concept indicated by the word "when", or actually using the word "when", lend themselves to an interpretation that the items identified following this "when" – the empty earth, the darkness, the deep and its surface, the Divine Presence/Spirit/Wind/Breath –

existed prior to what is considered the creative process that God is about to initiate. These items are the basic building materials for creation. Then comes the first utterance of "Let there be light" as the first act of creation.

Under either translation/interpretation, it is clear that the opening lines of Genesis are describing a process whereby unmanifest potentiality begins the process leading to actualization in manifestation. All potentiality originates from The One, and it would appear that even more primal than sound and light is earth, darkness, water and breath/spirit. If creation is defined as "bringing into manifestation", then it can be argued that the first manifestation is light, brought about by the first sound, the first utterance. Perhaps an utterance is a cause which will always have an effect, and as such, an utterance can never be a manifestation separate from its effect. The effect is the manifestation, the creation; and the first effect of the first sound is light.

On the third day, through an utterance, God gathered the waters below heaven in one place to allow for the appearance of dry land, called earth, "eretz", the same word used for the formless earth in the first sentence. So by gathering the water into one place, the formless earth, which was apparently formless because it was covered by or intermixed with water, now emerges and takes form. This is similar to the earlier recitation of the "formless" light existing in a diffused state within the darkness, becoming concentrated and separated from the darkness, thus giving light a more definitive form. One distinction, however, is that the separation of the dry earth from the wet water is accomplished through an utterance, while the separation of the light from the darkness is not conducted with an utterance.

Viewing these first three days of Genesis together, to try to conceive of some coherent scheme lends itself to an interpretation as follows. Genesis is a narration of a creation cycle consistent with Eastern models that existence goes through cycles of manifest creation back to unmanifest dissolution over and over again, similar to the "bang-bang" theory in physics. Alternatively, it is a description of the "big bang" theory for those who do not subscribe to the theory of repeating cycles. In the beginning of the one and only creation, or a creation cycle, the first potentialities appear, yet still in an unmanifested state. These potentialities include the primordial substance building materials for manifest creation of fire, water, earth, air/breath, sound and light. Along with Divine Will/Intent, these are all found in the opening sentences of Genesis describing the first day. Divine Will/Intent assembles these elements and impels them through the process of creation into manifestation. A key event is when light is separated from darkness, thus concentrating light, resulting in the "lightning flash" as described in Kabala, which initiates the process leading to creation as we know it, starting with the trees and the worlds. It is again worth noting that an utterance is not associated with this mysterious process of concentrating and separating the light. The operative verb, "yavdel" (used with the "and" prefix, "va": "vayavdel"), is usually translated as "separated" or "divided".

It appears that conceptions of a personalized God that we find in all different traditions exist within the realm of manifestation resulting from the initial lightning flash. But these elements, these aspects, these qualities of the unmanifest realm prior to the lightning flash, paradoxically don't remain and reside there; they are also permeating manifest creation all of the time. For some of us, these aspects of the unmanifest supply sufficient inspiration and spiritual connection. What many of the rabbis and teachers in other spiritual traditions have taught who acknowledge this is that it is all fine and good, but many people have trouble relating to Nothingness. You can't put your arms around it and get warm and fuzzy with the Void. People need something more anthropomorphic, so we have the deification of certain aspects at these other manifest levels. Theistic and pantheistic personalizations emerge because it is easier to relate to an abstraction such as Divinity if it is assigned some semblance of tangible being, with describable attributes and qualities, and perhaps even physical characteristics.

In Judaism, in the Vedic culture, people don't sit down in a synagogue or temple and pray to Brahman or the Ein or the Ein Soph. They pray to Jehovah/Yahweh/Hashem, they pray to Shiva or Vishnu or Krishna or some incarnation. You pray to something that is more personalized. You pray to the Shekinah or some other aspect of the Divine Mother. However, to be spiritually complete and balanced, we need to keep in mind the levels beyond personalization. This impersonal level exists in Judaism and in other traditions. Through meditation, you can connect with that level. That is an important point. The core spiritual experience from which all other things arise is a connection with that level. By connecting with that level, we attain purification to better function in the outer world. This is the most significant of all aspects of spirituality because it is the core, and the core, by definition, permeates, exists, throughout all of creation, and creation emanates out of it. The various qualities of consciousness don't exist only in a pre-emanated state. They exist throughout emanation, throughout creation, down to the lowliest, the grossest level of creation. The primary mystical experience, mystical conception, is that there is this thing that is referred to as consciousness, awareness, spirit, isness, beingness, that exists at all levels of creation. If it didn't, nothing could exist.

Judaism and Advaita Vedanta both emphasize Oneness, and to never forget the One. The essence of Oneness courses through everything, but particularly through the balancing influence of the middle pillar, the middle essence, where pure spirit can be most easily accessed. We are meant to climb up the middle of Jacob's Ladder, not the sides, for the middle is the Way. It is there to remind us that pure spirit is beyond and prior to light and sound and energy; it is That from which the Vedic primordial fire of Agni emanates, from where light and sound emanate. But it doesn't exist only in the beyond, it doesn't exist only prior to creation, it exists throughout creation, while creation is emanating. That is the idea that God is a verb. Part of the purity of pre-creation consciousness permeates everything all of the time. Nothing can exist without the middle pillar, nothing can exist without pure consciousness. Pure consciousness is the underlying medium through which everything exists. Without it, nothing exists. It is always present at all times.

There is nothing separate; there is a unity underlying apparent diversity. At one level, we perceive all of this diversity, this emanation and creation and the relative world, but underlying that is the unity that binds it all together. This element, quality, medium that we call "consciousness" makes all of this possible. It is our true primary medium through which we function. Not only is it a medium, consciousness is also a vehicle, a tool that can be utilized. When you connect with consciousness, you transcend the general laws of physics, of the relative world, including time and space. That is why it has been referred to as "the field of infinite possibilities". You can exist in more than one place at the same time. Time can stand still. Anything is possible when you are able to connect with that realm. That is the operating principle behind miracles and extraordinary powers associated with saints, sages and yogis in both the East and the West. These beings have tapped into this medium, this vehicle, and operate through it.

The Serpent Power

In the yoga system, although there has been some confusion about referring to kundalini shakti as a type of concentrated pranic energy, there is an alternative and more accurate view that it is a mysterious power of consciousness more subtle than and distinguished from energy. The basic conception is that the kundalini is akin to a serpent coiled and asleep at the base of the spine. In this slumbering static state, it contributes to the sustenance of basic life-functions and consciousness, but not much more. When the kundalini shakti is awakened and released, it moves up the middle channel, called "sushumna", correlated with the spine, enlivening the seven chakras along the way. If guided properly, it results not only in a higher level of functioning, but also in spiritual transformation. There are yoga practices addressing the process of this ascending force, which should be coordinated with a process of opening up and surrendering to the grace of the descending force, establishing a balanced approach to inner transformation. The image of a serpent or dragon is found among many traditions and myths ranging from China to Europe, including the Judeo-Christian tradition. The general view in this tradition, stemming from events concerning that dastardly serpent in the Garden of Eden, is that it provokes sin and evil-doing. After all, that primordial snake was punished accordingly by being made to slither on the ground at the lowest earthly level. That is the standard Judeo-Christian interpretation of those events, although there are slightly different implications and demarcations between the Jewish and Christian theologies. The Christian belief in Original Sin stems from this event, while Jewish thought does not recognize the doctrine of Original Sin, but rather that man has both positive and negative inclinations, and this was an example of being led into a negative path, but not Original Sin from which we must be saved.

I have not come across any Jewish sources, traditional or otherwise, presenting the kind of radically different interpretation of this event as taught in the Karin Kabalah course, although I have come across a very different sense of the meaning of the serpent power akin to the yogic view found in some Jewish mystical commentaries about another event later on in Exodus. The alternative interpretation concerning the Garden of Eden incident with the serpent is that it was emblematic of a primordial descent and awakening of the kundalini necessary for material life to involve and actualize. Life in the Garden contained subtle level prototypes for life outside the Garden, but life in the Garden was not in the physical realm as we know it. Expulsion from the Garden was tantamount to the birth of physicality as we know it. It had nothing to do with sin. It marked the final enshrining and activation of the kundalini power into the world of physicality which is essential for its sustained existence. The serpent was an agent of God carrying out God's plan to create physical manifestation. The "punishment", whereby the serpent became the lowliest creature slithering on the lowest level of the earth, is symbolic of the serpent's place as the originator and sustainer at the foundation of physicality.

As noted above, there is an event in the Exodus story, as interpreted by Jewish mystical sources, which ties in with this alternative view of the serpent. As we know, the Exodus story includes the events whereby Moses and Aaron go to Pharaoh and petition him to let the people go. They give Pharaoh all of these warnings of bad things that will befall him and Egypt if he doesn't let them go. A pattern develops whereby Pharaoh agrees and then changes his mind, resulting in the plagues. This leads up to the last straw event, the plague of the death of the first born. Unlike all of the other plagues that were carried out through the agency of mortal servants, this last plague is executed directly by the Lord of life and death.

The name of this Torah portion is "Bo". "Bo" means "come". In prior directives, God usually told Moses to "go". "Go" to Pharaoh and do this and this and say this and this. But this time, God says "come". As with the kind of detailed analysis of these texts involved in Jewish scholarship, this change in word usage for a similar event provoked questions. Why is God saying "come" this time instead of "go"? What is the significance to the word "come"? Well, the word "come" has a connotation that God is present with Pharaoh. God is saying, "Come to Pharaoh. I am here with Pharaoh." Not go. Come. "Go" connotes that God is with Moses, and God will go with Moses to see Pharaoh. But now there is this new twist where God is telling Moses to come see me and Pharaoh. I am present here with Pharaoh. Come see me in my presence with Pharaoh.

Images and depictions of Pharaoh include a serpent headdress. Pharaoh was the kingly ruler, the kingly expression of divinity on earth. His big crown was a serpent, a prevalent Egyptian image and another appearance of this widespread motif. The profound mystical commentary concerning this event is that Pharaoh was an example of bloated ego gone astray. He was the epitome of power on earth at that time, of activated but imbalanced kundalini straying way off course. His power expressed through the lower egoic self as prideful, arrogant domination, not humble service, as contrasted with and epitomized by Moses. Yoga maintains that the kundalini power in and of itself is neutral; it can be awakened, released and channeled productively or destructively, positively or negatively. They had magicians and occultists in Egypt, and Pharaoh was their overlord. He was like a Rasputin, an example of the kundalini gone terribly wrong.

The Jewish mystical interpretation of this event suggests that Moses was afraid to confront Pharaoh at this level, even though he had already confronted him on other levels. Now God was requiring Moses to penetrate to the essence of Pharaoh's power. It was important to address the core of that power and pierce it, transcend it, in order to overcome it and fulfill the mission of liberation. That power is not supposed to control your life; you're supposed to harness and direct it. When it starts controlling your life, becoming your life, you're going to stray onto a negative tangent. Pharaoh was a slave to his own power and thus he enslaved others, because that is all he knew. It was a personal challenge for Moses to navigate beyond the kundalini, the very essence of Pharaoh's power, and locate its source, where God resides. The narrative of the plagues makes it clear that Pharaoh was a mere puppet in God's hands; God "hardened" Pharaoh's heart, prompting him to change his mind, although Pharaoh thought he was acting on his own volition. Moses needed to discover the Puppeteer behind the puppet. To succeed, a liberator must first experience liberation. That is why God said, "come". Come and see why you have to pierce through Pharaoh's power, come and see Me as its source. Know the essence of liberation, and that will be the final straw leading to a successful mission. It is a powerful rendition and interpretation of that story.

Chapter Six

Life, Death and Breath
The Mandukya Upanishad, Yogic Sleep and Conscious Death
The Enlightened Life, the Life of The Tzaddik

Life, Death and Breath

Death is a subject that all spiritual teachings address, although many people don't want to talk about it. The general teaching is that you can't master, enjoy and express life to its fullest unless you address death. Of course, we're all going to address death when we die. The idea is to address the fact that we are going to die in a conscious, intentional manner while we are still alive. The more thoroughly and completely we can address it and have a real sense of it, the better equipped we will be when that eventuality occurs. It will also equip us to enjoy life more, because overcoming the fear of death makes us fearless, and fearlessness is a quality extolled by spiritual teachers. The argument continues that you cannot be totally fearless and thus you cannot totally enjoy life unless you address death on some level or another, the more comprehensive, the better. Spiritual teachers from varying traditions have expressed that you cannot conquer life until you conquer death. One key to unlocking the mysteries of life and death is breath.

Taking a look at Genesis, we find that God breathed life into Adam. The breath of life was breathed into the nostrils of androgynous man. God's exhalation is man's inhalation. Life begins with God's exhalation and our inhalation. The opposite also applies: God's inhalation is our exhalation. We refer to dying as expiring. "Expire" comes from the Latin root, "spire", which means breathing or breath, and it is also the root for the term "spirit". When we talk about church spires, inspiration, we are referring to breathing, to spirit; inspiration is breathing in: when we are inspired, it is caused by the spirit within becoming enlivened. When we expire, we breath our last. We have the phrase, "he breathed his last", "she expired". When we expire, it is on our exhalation, with God taking us back through His inhalation. What a profound and beautiful expression of this process!

There are several examples in the Torah illustrating various conceptions of death, the dying process, and the quality of that process depending upon the spiritual advancement of the individual involved. There are narrations describing people passing away in a "normal" mortal fashion, and then once in a while, someone passes away in a different and special fashion such as "walking with God". Fairly early in Genesis, Enoch is the first one. There is a list of a lineal descent recited: and so-and-so lived and died, and so-and-so lived and died, but then there is a break in that pattern, when the text states, "and Enoch lived, and then he walked with God". It doesn't say "died" like the others recited before him. There was something different about Enoch. One interpretation is that Enoch didn't die a physical bodily death like the others; instead, he "walked with God", as did the prophets upon their deaths.

Well, what is the meaning and significance of this "walking with God"? It's described as a way of re-entering the Garden of Eden, gaining entry past the shield, sword and flame that protects Paradise. Somehow, there is a physical, bodily entrance into the Garden. That is also the method for obtaining the gift of prophecy: prophets enter the Garden, receive their revelations, and then come back, re-enter the world, and deliver their prophecies. One theory is that Enoch became the prophet Elijah, who is also the Archangel Metatron.

When someone "walks with God" when they die, they supposedly are able to enter Eden/Paradise with their body and soul intact. They don't physically drop the body with their soul leaving the body as it occurs in "normal" dying. As an alternative to this view, I prefer an interpretation more in keeping with the idea of consciously dying in the yogic sense. When an accomplished yogi dies through the process called "maha samadhi", they consciously leave their bodies, but it's still leaving the body. We're so materially oriented that the traditional interpretation is that Enoch physically, bodily went back, but my view is that his inner wholeness rendered his leaving the body in a pleasant, gradual manner, because he had achieved the state that yogis achieve when they're able to attain maha samadhi. It is not the fearful kind of thing that most people experience when they die, an involuntary separation of the body from what remains after the body ceases to function.

This view of the dying process of "walking with God" is more consistent with another phrase found in Jewish sources designating a process of the graceful exiting of life achieved by the prophets: leaving the earth through the agency of "death by Divine Kiss". The image of God kissing hearkens back to the discussion earlier in this chapter that as God kisses you, God inhales and draws that life force out of you permanently, or for that particular worldly existence. Of course, the image of God breathing life into the nostrils of man could also be described as a Divine Kiss of God's exhalation bequeathing life, but I have not found that usage in the sources; the references are to a process of dying.

There is yet another description of conscious dying by advanced beings in the Torah tradition. There is discussion about the great sages, like Moses and

Abraham, and how they died. In these discussions, there is a sense of them dying and leaving their bodies, unlike the conception discussed above of physically, bodily rising to heaven. There is a comparison made with a common person who leaves their body involuntarily because they are not spiritually evolved or prepared for conscious death. The image in such a case is that the dying process is likened to a burr being removed from the fur of an animal. There is a difficult, unpleasant, somewhat violent ripping away. There is a part of a regular mortal person who is trying to cling to life with all they've got. All of our medical sciences focus on trying to keep a dying person alive, often accompanied by the dying person desperately clinging to life, attempting to avoid the horror they perceive as the prospect of death. But if it's your time, that burr is going to get ripped from the fur. These same commentaries say that for a highly evolved being like Moses, the image is that the dying process is like a strand of hair being removed from a cup of milk. The soul is easily extricated and moves on. That's the difference in the quality of the dying, depending upon how evolved a being is. So the sages, prophets and more advanced souls exit through the mechanisms of the Divine Kiss, of Walking with God, like a hair being removed from a cup of milk. The rest of us slobs exit through the mechanism of the burr being pulled out from the fur!

In the yoga system, there is a connection between breath and prana. Prana is this subtle life force that flows with the breath, functions along with the breath, but operates on a finer, a more subtle level than the biochemical processes involved with breathing. That is why in yoga, breathing exercises – the science of breath – is also called "pranayama", the understanding, control and direction, not only of the breath, but of the prana. In yoga, there are layers, sheaths, called "koshas" surrounding the soul that lies within an individual. The outermost layer is the physical layer of the body. The next level in is the pranic layer. This prana, this breath, is the layer connecting our outer material world with our inner world. It is a significant intermediary level. Prana flows. The prana flows through a system of subtle channels that generally correspond with the nervous system, but apparently there are more pranic channels, called "nadis", than the total of all of the branches of the nervous system. It is the flowing of that prana that energizes us. It gives us life.

Mystical Judaism describes a correspondence between the 613 commandments (see the Appendix) and inner subtle energy channels (some sources focus more on the 248 positive commandments corresponding to 248 primary "organs" of the body). By observing the commandments, you are enlivening the related inner energy channels and organs. It sounds remarkably similar to the yogic description of the "nadis", the pranic channels. The sources disagree as to their exact number, but all claim that there are thousands of nadis.

When prana stops flowing, we're dead. One definition of death is the cessation of breath. If you stop breathing for a certain period of time, if your prana stops flowing for a certain period of time, you're going to be dead. In advanced yoga breathing practices, there is intentional breath retention, on both inhalation and exhalation. It appears that the preliminary steps towards learning how to consciously die – like a strand of hair being removed from a cup of milk, rather than like a burr being removed from the fur of an animal – involves mastering the breath, that whole pranic process. It results in being more in control and knowing what is happening with your body, knowing that it is time to leave, and being able to consciously control or follow the ceasing of the flow of prana. When you consciously control it, or at least are consciously aware of the process happening, then you can consciously leave the body. If you're not consciously aware or controlling, it's going to happen anyway, but it's going to be more like the burr than the strand of hair, and you will be swept into a state of deep unconsciousness.

There are yogic practices where advanced yogis can leave a body and come back. I believe this is all related to advanced breathing and pranayama techniques. A lot of it probably has to do with controlling the prana, slowing it down, even temporarily stopping it, or stopping it for longer than we commonly believe would be imaginable, where that sheath is left in a static state and the rest of the soul goes elsewhere and does what it does and then comes back to the body. But in maha samadhi, the final exit of no return, you leave the body, drop the body, and the body is gone. This is some preliminary food for thought about addressing death and the mechanisms involved in consciously dying.

The Mandukya Upanishad, Yogic Sleep and Conscious Death

Swami Rama identified certain sacred texts that were particularly important to our tradition. The Mandukya Upanishad is one such text, and it has always been one of my favorites. Basically, the Mandukya Upanishad is an explanation of the mantra, AUM. AUM is often spelled in English and pronounced with just an "O" and an "M": "OM". But sometimes it is also spelled and pronounced "A", "U", "M": "AUM", "Ahh OO MM." The text is an explication of what "AUM" really means and signifies, basic levels of consciousness existing in the manifest and unmanifest realms.

We often talk about "raising" our consciousness, "altered" states of consciousness, "higher" and "lower" consciousness. What, after all, is consciousness? Pure consciousness involves through the various levels of existence, becoming covered by veils, enclosed within sheaths. The pure consciousness, from one point of view, remains pure. But it becomes filtered by

90

the veils, the sheaths. Those filters effectuate an apparent lowering of the consciousness, but at some level, that consciousness remains pure. If your primary focus is at the level of a certain filter, it seems like a lower level because it is being filtered, covered, veiled.

The Mandukya Upanishad says that the "A" in "AUM" stands for the waking state, the "U" stands for the dreaming state, and the "M" stands for the state of dreamless sleep. But then there is the dot-dot-dot following the "M", "AUM..." which carries on into Infinity and the Void. That dot-dot-dot leads to what is called the fourth state, the state of "Turiya", which is the state beyond, the level of existence beyond the layers, at the level of the unmanifest realm.

A distinction and relationship needs to be made between states of *mind* and states of *consciousness*. While the Mandukya Upanishad focuses on states of consciousness, another important text in the Yoga tradition, the Yoga Sutras of Patanjali, focuses on states of mind. In Chapter Four, we described the structure and functions of the mind according to Yoga, and that the mind is referred to as the "inner instrument", just as the body is the outer instrument. They are *instruments* of consciousness, but they *are not the same as* consciousness. One definition of "Samadhi", the end-point of yoga practice, is a state of quiet mind. Another description of samadhi is "absorption", when the mind becomes fully absorbed. What is the mind fully absorbed with or in? Consciousness. When quiet mind is achieved, it becomes the threshold of the doorway leading to what is beyond the mind and all manifest existence, Turiya, the Fourth State of consciousness. So quieting the mind, Samadhi, provides the mind a vision of the Unspeakable Beyond, and allows the self entry into Turiya, the state of pure, unadulterated consciousness.

One tenet of this teaching is that Turiya is not a state that can only be attained when you are sitting in meditation, although certainly sitting meditation is a powerful and useful tool to both attain it and cultivate it. Once you attain and develop this state, and it grows within you, at some point, it can exist simultaneously while the other states also exist. It is always existing simultaneously anyway, but, generally, we're not aware of it. When our awareness becomes entrenched enough in Turiya, we realize that this level and quality of being exists all the time, regardless of anything else, because it is permanent. Everything else, all other states, are impermanent and transitory. Turiya is the state of permanence. This Turiya level of consciousness can exist simultaneously with waking, dreaming, and deep dreamless sleep. There is a part of us that never sleeps. There is a part of us that is, as the scriptures state, "ever pure, ever wise, ever free," and these other layers exist on top of that. If we can establish our identity at that higher level, then we can see that all of those other things are occurring while that permanent state remains. That is a definition of "meditation in action". It also provides an explanation behind the phenomenon that is called "lucid dreaming". In lucid dreaming, there is a part of you that is aware you are dreaming while you are dreaming. The part of you that is aware that you are dreaming while you are dreaming is that place that never sleeps, a detached observer state of being.

That has been the general explication through the Mandukya Upanishad of these four basic states of consciousness associated with the syllables of the "AUM" mantra. However, I had an opportunity to view video tapes of a seminar that Swami Rama once conducted on the Mandukya Upanishad in which he made reference to three additional states of consciousness. He described them as states of transition experienced as one shifts from one of the primary four into another. In other words, there is a transitional state between waking and dreaming, between dreaming and deep sleep, and between deep sleep and the fourth state, Turiya. He said if you get trapped in the state between waking and dreaming, you can go mad. It is like a state of psychosis, schizophrenia, because it is a state which blurs dreaming and wakefulness, inner fantasy and imaginings and outer reality. At the time I viewed these videos, I had recently seen the movie "A Beautiful Mind" [reference to a movie about a brilliant genius who suffered the mental illness of psychosis]. This provided an explanation for what that poor man was going through, because his waking reality was blurred with his dream state. He had no sense of what was physically real and what was something that was an imagining in his mind only. He was caught and stuck in that state. He couldn't discern what was real and what wasn't real on the physical, outer level. He said he was never cured, but rather that he just got used to it. There were certain recurring personages who were figments of his imagination who seemed real to him. He trained himself to ignore them, knowing through what he had endured that they didn't exist in the outside world, even though perceptually he couldn't make that distinction. He didn't give them attention, he didn't give them energy, so they just remained as background nuisances. This sounds like a process similar to how we are supposed to regard our chattering mind during meditation, to get beyond it. We are instructed to ignore the thoughts, sounds and images of our mind and thus not energize them. He never really got over his problem, he just got used to it and could therefore function productively once again. There is a touching scene towards the end of the movie when a person informs him that he has been nominated for a Nobel prize. He turns to a student of his and asks, "Is this person I'm talking to over here a real person?" He isn't sure. He thinks maybe it is a new personage that is a figment of his imagination. His student confirms that the person is really there, that it isn't one of his imaginings, it isn't one of his psychotic experiences. That's why Swami Rama frequently emphasized that it is not healthy to fantasize too much without action, lest our fantasy world takes over and becomes our reality.

Swami Rama said that the state in between dreaming and deep sleep is the state of prophetic revelation. It is different than the individual psychotic imaginings of the state described above, and it is different than the normal dream state, although it may be confused with the normal dream state, as it also occurs during sleep. It is a state where you can access deeper spiritual images and messages and prophetic revelation. The quality of such experiences is distinct from normal dreams.

Whenever Swami Rama spoke about Turiya, he often talked about how deep dreamless sleep and Turiya were actually very similar. You are close to Turiya when you are in deep sleep because in deep dreamless sleep, your mind is quiet, opening access to pure consciousness, just as in Turiya. The problem is that you enter and experience deep sleep while you are unconscious, so you aren't aware of what you are close to. When you enter Turiya, you enter it consciously, and that makes all the difference in the world. When you enter it consciously, you are aware of it, and you can gain the benefit from it in ways not available through normal unconscious deep dreamless sleep. When you enter it unconsciously, you don't gain as much benefit, although you get some good rest. By entering it consciously, you get even a deeper rest and benefits. Swami Rama often noted that he thought it a strange Western custom to wish someone "sweet dreams", because dreaming sleep, even with good dreams, does not provide good, deep rest. We get better rest in dreamless sleep, but in Turiya, we get the best rest.

He called the last transitional realm between unconscious deep dreamless sleep and Turiya "Yoga Nidra", yogic sleep. Subsequent teachings from him directly and through his successor teachers after his passing, have further expounded on yoga nidra and its significance. At some point, I came to realize that I had been having experiences of this state over a number of years, but I had no point of reference to understand or identify it. I have found when I describe it in meditation classes I conduct, there usually are a few other people who have likewise had such experiences. I used to call this experience a "frozen state" episode because of what I experienced. It usually occurred during the day when I would take a little cat nap. I would fall asleep, but then, all of a sudden, I would wake up. However, I realized that I had not woken up to my normal waking state, because my body was still asleep. I called it "frozen" as I could literally feel something like a paralysis in my body. I eventually realized it felt that way because my body was still asleep; but I was awake, inside my sleeping body, perfectly awake. I could feel this force, the force of sleep keeping my eyelids closed, and my body was at perfect peace. It was not restless at all. It was just working at a minimum "autopilot" sleep level, being perfectly at peace, perfectly still. My mind was also more still than normal. It was like the mind was also functioning at a minimal level, but I was aware and awake. I was aware of sounds in the room and of being in my body. But my mind wasn't doing its normal chit-chat. It was very quiet and still. There was this sense of deep rest and peace, yet being awake at the same time. There were times that I felt like I was actually being visited while in that state, as if teachers from another realm, on another level, were visiting. I could sense a physical presence. There were even times when I actually felt a robe brush against me. I knew there wasn't someone physically with a robe in the room, but on some other equally real level, there was someone with a robe who brushed by me. I knew that I was being looked after and being given some kind of guidance in this state. Then eventually, through Swami Rama's teachings and descriptions of yoga nidra that began to emerge, I made the connection that my "frozen state" episodes were experiences of yoga nidra.

Swami Rama has elaborated that there are actually many different levels and forms of yoga nidra. The basic experience is your body is asleep, but your mind, your inner consciousness is totally awake and aware. Usually, when you fall asleep, your body falls asleep, and your mind, your normal conscious mind falls asleep too. That is when you may have dreams, but this mental activity is occurring while you are unconscious. In yoga nidra, the body is asleep, but the mind doesn't go to sleep. Or the mind goes asleep momentarily, but suddenly you wake up, not to normal wakefulness, but your mind wakes up inside your body that remains asleep. In his descriptions of how to attain the state of yoga nidra, Swami Rama directs that when you think you're about to go to sleep, try not to go to sleep, and at that juncture of "twilight" sleep — of being half-awake and half asleep — you might shift into that state. My personal experience has been slightly different. It seems as if I fall asleep, and all of a sudden, something snaps/shifts, and I wake up, but I don't wake up to my normal waking state; I wake up to my mind being awake, but not my body. So my body is still asleep, and I realize that I'm in my body, and my body is just there.

Residing in the state of yoga nidra provides a profound experience and insight into the notion that you are not your body; your body is part of what you are, but there is a part of you beyond your body. Yoga teaches that the material body is the outermost layer covering the soul, that the next layer in is the pranic layer, followed by the mind layer, and that prana is the link between the body and the mind. It is one thing to have an intellectual understanding of that on an intellectual level. But yoga nidra is an experiential mode of realizing it. You are in your body, your body is asleep, and you're awake. It is a much more profound level of experiencing that you are not your body. Your body is barely there. It is just asleep. You become profoundly aware of your breath; it comes front and center. But it is the very gentle, quiet breathing of a sleeping person. Swami Rama says that the breathing can become very quiet. It makes you acutely aware of the breathing/pranic level, of that inner energy level that is connecting your body to your mind.

One significance to me of yoga nidra is that it is related to the Jewish conceptions of how the sages died and "walked with God", the "Divine Kiss", the method of dying and leaving the earth similar to a hair being drawn from a glass of milk as opposed to dying and leaving the earth like a burr being ripped from the fur of an animal. The breath comes to the fore while the body recedes, and the breath becomes very still and quiet. God's exhalation is what brings us to life, as God breathed life into man. This step of yoga nidra helps us prepare for that day when God's inhalation will take that life back to Himself. We're "walking with God", we're being brought back to God; God's inhalation is our exhalation. On our final exhalation, our "expiration", we've "expired", we've "breathed our last"; our breath is released and our prana is recycled back to God. In yoga nidra, the most refined level of our mind — the quiet mind — stands intact at the threshold of the door leading to Turiya, Pure Consciousness, the Ultimate Source of Creation. Swami Rama has said in that state, any questions we have will be answered, as we encounter the Source of All. In samadhi, the mind passes through the door and temporarily dissolves; there is no mind left to formulate any question.

To expand on this further, it appears that yoga nidra is a significant first step towards learning how to die consciously. Just as there is a qualitative difference between unconscious deep sleep and conscious deep sleep (Turiya), there is a similar qualitative difference between losing consciousness when you die and retaining consciousness when you die. "Walking with God", "death by the Divine Kiss" is like consciously dying. I have read many stories about Swami Rama and other sages and accomplished yogis he practiced with being able to consciously attain death. It is similar to the idea that even when we go to sleep, a part of us remains awake; even when we bodily die, a part of us remains awake. Yoga nidra demonstrates to us that we can physically, bodily be asleep while yet another part of us remains awake. Conscious death is a deeper correlate. If we can remain awake and alert while our body remains asleep, perhaps we can remain awake and alert when our body permanently dies. We can bodily die while another part of us does not die.

To truly master life, one needs to master death. Mastering death is being able to consciously leave your body when it is time for your body to cease functioning. Yoga nidra is the first step, because you are now acutely aware of the fact that you are not your body. Now you are becoming aware of your pranic level, your energy level, that connects your body to your mind. The lower aspect of your normal waking mind is barely there because it is still asleep. There is a more subtle part of you, your higher mind and your consciousness, that is still awake. If you take that a few steps further, then you are ready to consciously leave the body when the body is ready to drop. You can bid goodbye to the body, goodbye to the breath, and still be awake during that process. What we call death, when it is done in consciousness like this, is called going into "Maha Samadhi" in yoga – consciously leaving the body when it is no longer useful and ceases to function. At the same time, something else "passes on", "passes away", phrases we also use in describing death consistent with the conception that not everything dies. Something remains functioning, passing on, passing away to another realm.

The Enlightened Life, The Life of The Tzaddik

Figure 4 at the end of this chapter depicts what I call the "bullseye" chart, as it is a series of 5 concentric circles. The enumeration under the heading, "The Inner Stroke" is one yogic depiction of the layers of our being. At the center is pure unadulterated spirit/consciousness, which we have discussed elsewhere in some detail. The ever larger circles emanating out from the center indicate the sheaths, coverings, veils that surround the pure inner consciousness. Some mystic traditions talk about rending, parting, piercing "veils". They are referring to these sheaths that are called "koshas" in yoga. Moving out from the center, the spaces in between each sheath indicate gradations of consciousness, having been filtered by the sheaths that precede each level. As you move out from the center, each successive level of consciousness gets increasingly filtered until you reach the outermost level of consciousness outside the last sheath. The first innermost sheath is called the "anandamaya kosha", the "blissful sheath"; "ananda" means bliss. This first sheath reflects the Ananda, the Bliss from the Realm Beyond, the realm of Sat Chit Ananda. The next level is "vijnanamaya kosha", the layer of the higher mind, the discriminating, discerning mind, elsewhere defined as the "buddhi". Then we have the lower mind, the "manomaya kosha", elsewhere defined as "manas". Then there is the prana, the pranic sheath, the "pranamaya kosha". The final sheath, which is the physical body of matter, is the "annamaya kosha", the food level. So each one of those layers, sheaths, coverings, veils, enclose and filter the inner pureness. If our attention is focused at the physical layer, we have a bodily consciousness. There appear to be differences in the qualities of consciousness at each of these levels. Even though consciousness permeates all, consciousness gets veiled/filtered.

Spiritual process, meditative process, is intended to connect with the innermost pure consciousness that exists in its pureness to a small degree even at the outermost level despite all of the filters. It can be difficult to see through these filters, pierce through these veils and connect with the pure kernel which still exists beneath all of these layers. The more we can do that, the more we can bring "meditation into action", and the more we can purify ourselves, scrub those layers and at least make them more translucent, more transparent. Maybe we can't make them totally clear, because they still function, but they can function on a clearer, cleaner level than they normally do, because there is a lot of schmutz, crud, dirt that collects on them. Part of the magic of the meditation process is that by connecting with a small kernel of this purity, it cleanses, it purifies all of these layers, and makes them more translucent, more transparent. This purification provides for the inner level to be better expressed and become a bigger part of who we are, what we are, and how we are functioning. So instead of it being maybe 2% of our everyday consciousness, and we are not even aware it is there, it becomes 10% or 15%, and we're aware that it is there. We begin to function in outer life while remaining more frequently connected with inner purity. At some point, a connection is established that remains without getting broken. A new level of functioning is attained: a part of us remains awake even when we're asleep; spiritual transformation is accelerated.

To go back to the subject of yoga nidra, usually, when we're asleep, we're unconscious on the physical, pranic, and mental levels. We're gone. That is because usually, something we know as our sense of identity, our egoic sense of separate self, is tied up with those levels. When we are asleep, we are not consciously awake or aware. The amount of this purer, deeper consciousness is too small to be retained consciously. Through yogic sleep, we're asleep at the physical level, but we're awake at the pranic and mind levels. We're acutely aware that the physical body is asleep, but the prana and the mind are still functioning, are awake. The process of consciously dying would be a matter of increasing the amount of wakeful consciousness at the inner levels, withdrawing the sense of identity from the outer levels. Yoga says that when the soul leaves the body, what survives are the three inner sheaths, which also includes the citta, the storehouse of all of the impressions from our past experiences, our samskaras, our karma. Those inner subtle impressions impel us back to reincarnate in order to take care of unfinished business. The new incarnation develops the outer layers again for the new physical being, influenced by the impressions that have been carried over. When our identity is firmly enough established at the inner layers, it can let go of the outer layers, say goodbye and move along into another body. Part of what we are continues, another part permanently expires and returns to the dust of the earth. The true Self remains. The True Self is beyond the usual separative ego. When our identity resides with this deeper True Self beyond the usual ego, we are living more realized lives, and we get close to the point where we can consciously leave the body and consciously reincarnate.

There is another way of looking at this bullseye chart. As described above, it conveys a sense that our pure essence, what in Western mysticism is called our "monad", our spark of divinity, is this little "spark" that is barely discernible, covered and distorted by the multiple layers surrounding it. This is a traditional model utilized in yoga and employed on a regular basis by Swami Rama in his teachings. This is consistent with the description I have provided of yoga nidra, whereby there is a sense that the mind remains awake inside the sleeping body. However, Swami Rama has said that there are several forms of yoga nidra, and he would also frequently emphasize that *the entire body is contained within the mind, but the entire mind is not contained within the body*. In the bullseye depiction as I have first presented it, the mind is contained within the body; it appears that the mind and the soul are contained within the body. But then, what about the assertion that the entire mind is not contained within the body?

At a certain level of awareness, we have a sense that we are a body, our mind is inside our body, and our spirit is something even deeper and smaller, this little kernel of something somewhere deep inside. We have a conception of this physical model that everything is contained within our body. But then along comes this other viewpoint that the entire body is contained within the mind, not the other way around. Well, that suggests a whole different orientation to this scheme. It suggests that everything should be reversed, with the largest circle becoming the blissful sheath and the smallest inner circle becoming the bodily sheath, as depicted in the enumeration in Figure 4 under the heading of "The Outer Stroke". What lies beyond the outermost circle is pure unadulterated consciousness, and what lies within the center is the constricted bodily consciousness. It is based upon a point of view. If you are really connected with spirit, with unity, you see that your body is just an element immersed in this incredible vast unity. Your spirit is not just this little kernel or flame or spark of something deep within, but you are connected with the Universal Spirit that is everywhere, that is our medium, that unifies everything. Our bodies are just these elements, not much more than apparitions, outlines, double exposures, immersed in this vast ocean of Spirit.

To continue with this water metaphor, do you have a sense that your spirit is an ocean or a drop of water? When you feel that your spirit is just a little drop of ocean water, you're in the first model. When you realize that drop of ocean water is connected to the vastness of the cosmic ocean, then you're in the second model. In the Yoga Vedanta system, it corresponds with what is described as the realization that the Atman, the pure individual self within, is actually one with the Brahman, the pure Universal Self.

So there are these different phases to our spiritual development that can be called "the inner stroke" and the "outer stroke". Meditative teachings often describe the development of awareness as going "within". You start with this bodily level, quiet the body, regulate the breath/prana, quiet the mind and eventually contact the little inner droplet inside. This process involves examining and reevaluating our sense of self, of identity. What do we think we are, who do we think we are? In the yoga tradition, there is the ego, the ahamkara, this sense of self separate from others. When that sense of identity can merge with this inner spark, with this inner droplet of ocean water — the more that sense of self realizes, experiences it really is one and the same as this inner drop of water — all of a sudden the inner drop of water starts expanding. The sense that it is just an inner drop of water begins to merge with an experiential revelation that it is part of a vast ocean; a quantitative and qualitative shift begins to occur. That process is what can be called "the outer stroke". The sense of separate self becomes more like an apparition. It's just a little outline, a double exposure, that is moving through, superimposed upon the vastness of creation. There is a sense of being immersed in this vastness as opposed to being a little drop here, and there is another little drop there. There is no longer a here and a there.

Another common metaphor using water speaks of waves. If your consciousness is at the tip of a wave, and you're not even aware of your connection with the ocean, and you look out from the tip of a wave, what you see are other tips of other waves. Although the waves are comprised of the ocean, if each individual only has a sense of being a tip of a wave, they barely have a sense of what is lower down in the wave, containing a greater quantity of water and the greater power associated with it, let alone what is at the base of the wave connecting with the ocean, the origin of the waves. All they see is separation, because they can't even conceive of anything beyond it, even their own source. Through meditation you can start moving deeper. If you eventually get to the source, you just see sameness, you see unity everywhere. Up at the top of the waves, you see something a little similar, there is another human being, but you're here and they're there. When you are at the level below the individual waves, you may still have some sense that you're here and they're there, but you also see that there's hardly any difference. The difference is much less and begins to disappear. From that perspective, we can meet Swami Rama's challenge "to live in the world, yet remain above". "Living in the world" is seeing that there is a part of us that still has some sense of separation. "Remaining above" also realizes that we have this connection. So we can function in the world at the level of separation, but also remain in touch with the level of connection. Remaining in touch with the level of connection enhances the entire quality of what we do at the level of separation. When we're disconnected, because that is as far as our awareness goes, we're going to function much differently than if we sense the deeper connection.

FIGURE 4 – THE BULLSEYE

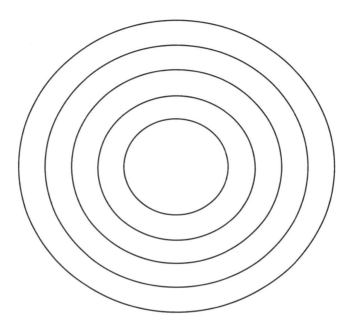

The Inner Stroke
Ordering of the rings/layers from the
largest to the smallest

1. Annamaya kosha – the food/body layer
2. Pranamaya kosha – the prana/vital force layer
3. Manomaya kosha – the lower mind layer
4. Vijnanamaya kosha – the higher mind layer
5. Anandamaya kosha – the blissful layer

The innermost space is the center of the pure
Self and unadulterated consciousness lying deep
within. The spaces in-between each layer are
levels of consciousness filtered by the sheaths in
proximity. The outermost space beyond the
largest ring is usual waking consciousness
accompanied by a sense of separation from
everything else. There is little sense of any
unity underlying the separate states of waking,
dreaming and dreamless sleep. Atman, the inner
Self, and Brahman, universal consciousness, are
perceived as separate.

The Outer Stroke
Ordering of the rings/layers from the
largest to the smallest

1. Anandamaya kosha – the blissful layer
2. Vijnanamaya kosha – the higher mind layer
3. Manomaya kosha – the lower mind layer
4. Pranamaya kosha – the prana/vital force layer
5. Annamaya kosha – the food/body layer

All spaces are permeated by a sense of unified
consciousness, with the sheaths and their filtering
effects perceived as double-exposed images superimposed upon the underlying all-pervading
Oneness. Waking, dreaming and dreamless sleep
are experienced and perceived as occurring within
a perspective of underlying unity of the fourth
state, Turiya. Atman and Brahman are perceived
as One.

Chapter Seven

One God, Many Names and Attributes

A central theme and subject in Judaism is that there is one God. In fact, Judaism claims to be the first religion teaching monotheism. Jewish emphasis on one inseparable God, along with the dictate against graven images, has led most Jewish thinkers to be critical of systems like Hindu pantheism, which utilize images and statues depicting embodiments of various gods and goddesses. For Jewish thinkers, that's idolatry, plain and simple. Nevertheless, in Judaism, there are many names, aspects, attributes, designations and qualities attributed to this one God, which seems to be a principle similar to the one upon which Hindu pantheism is based. A big distinction is that Hinduism extends it further by anthropomorphizing different aspects and incorporating their energies into depicted images, a practice abhorred not only by Judaism, but also by Islam and early Christianity.

In any case, one of the central names and figures for God, and one of the biggest mysteries in all of Judaism throughout the ages, has been the Tetragrammaton. "Tetragrammaton" is Greek for "four-letter word". The four Hebrew letters comprising this word are Yod Heh Vav Heh, YHVH [phonetic transliterations are cumbersome and imprecise, varying considerably in the Hebrew-to-English literature]. This is one of the main names, aspects, qualities for God used frequently in the Torah, although there are others, such as "Elohim", another significant designation often translated as "Creator". But YHVH is still considered *the* most central one because it is the one primarily representing Mercy, the right side of the Tree of Life, although it is also used in other ways. For example, it sometimes signifies the entire Tree descending down the middle. It also symbolizes the four worlds with its four letters, and it exists in different layers within each world. There are many connotations and permutations of this word and its letters, including employing them in breathing and meditation techniques.

There are conflicting views concerning the pronunciation of this word. One common notion is that there is no known pronunciation; it is an unsolved mystery. Another conception is that there is a known pronunciation, but the method to properly intone and pronounce it without profaning it is saved for an inner circle of prepared students. Certainly, one wouldn't want this word to be used in vain, as it is very special. There are many permutations from this same four-lettered Hebrew word; Yahweh and Jehovah are two common derivatives. The Jehovah's Witnesses say God's name is Jehovah, which name is meant to be proclaimed. There are no "J" or "W" sounds in traditional Hebrew, but there have been many changes over the years. Apparently, the "Y", in becoming anglicized, morphed into a "J" sound, and an ancient sounding of "Vav" was like a "W", although it morphed into the common present pronunciation of a "V". There is a slippery and sliding slope concerning the pronunciation of biblical Hebrew.

One interesting aspect to Hebrew is that the consonants are the main letters. The vowels are just these little markings underneath or on top of the consonants. The Torah scroll only contains consonants. Somehow, through the oral tradition, the vowels that accompanied those consonants were taught, although there are issues about which are the proper vowels. So the consonants for YHVH are clear, but the question is, what are the vowels? What is the proper pronunciation/intonation of this word, this most holy of all of the Jewish designations for a name/aspect/quality of God? I discovered one compelling explanation from a day spent with husband-and-wife Jewish Renewal Rabbis Arthur Waskow and Phyllis Berman: the sound of this word is the sound of breathing. This word is intricately intertwined with life and breath. Breathing, both Divine and human, is the process by which human life originates and is sustained. That is why breathing is such an important focal point of yóga practice, for it is an entry point to and connection with the Divine Realm. It is not just the physical biochemical breathing process involving the oxygenation of the blood and the elimination of carbon dioxide through the lungs. Yoga maintains that the essential life force, prana, rides with the breath, which is why breathing exercises, pranayama, are such an important focus in yoga practice. In the chapter on Jewish Yoga Meditation in this book, there is a detailed meditation technique employing these principles.

In the Torah, the first word to refer to God, in which God is really referring to Himself, is "Elohim". Elohim is basically left pillar, formation, which makes sense because Genesis, the beginning, is addressing formation of the world; God the Creator would be Elohim and not YHVH, which is pure force, because force cannot do anything without form. Further along in the text, the Tetragrammaton, YHVH, is introduced, another name utilized by God in referring to Him/Her/Itself. There then follow times when YHVH and Elohim are used separately and in conjunction with each other. I have not discovered or discerned any patterns or explanations for these variations. However, usually when they are used together, YHVH comes first, which makes sense because according to the lightning spark initiating manifest creation, it starts at the right side and then proceeds to the left. Form cannot do anything without force, force is useless without form, but force enlivens form. So usually the conjoined order will be YHVH Elohanu ("Elohanu" being a possessive derivative of Elohim).

In some circles, when people are speaking about God, they will often utilize "Hashem" as a reference to YHVH. "Hashem" means "The Name"; "Ha", "The", "Shem", "Name". A practice evolved some time ago that whenever the Tetragrammaton is depicted, whether in the Torah or in prayers, it will be depicted with those four consonants, but it will be pronounced "Adonoi". My childhood training led me to believe that "Adonoi" was just a substitute word for YHVH, because we were taught to use it that way, and I didn't discover until my adult return to study that it is also a word in its own right, used independently and spelled out as "Adonoi" with its own consonants and vowels. Whereas "Elohim" and "YHVH" are used by God referring to Him/Her/Itself, "Adonoi" is significant as being the first word used by a person, Abraham, in addressing God. So it is another level down, as it is man referring to God. However, we were taught that even though it is used as a substitute for the inutterable YHVH, Adonoi in and of itself was so sacred that when we were only practicing prayers and not reciting them in a real worship setting, it was substituted with "Adoshem". Likewise, the word "Elohanu", which is a possessive derivative of "Elohim", meaning "our Elohim", was considered too sacred to recite during practice sessions, so we would say "Elokanu". So in practice, it was "Adoshem Elokanu". But when we were doing the real thing in a real service, we had to remember to say "Adonoi Elohanu". That's how I learned it.

Other names, designations, attributes of the One God:

Hayah Hoveh V'Yeheyeh: "He was, He is and He will be". This phrase is derived from the Tetragrammaton, signifying the timelessness and eternal nature of God.

Ehyeh Asher Ehyeh: "I am That I am" or "I shall be as I shall be". In Moses' first encounter with God, when Moses was finally persuaded to take on the role to lead the Israelites out of Egypt, he asked God who he should say had sent him. This was the name God instructed Moses to tell them, that "I am" had sent him, which is similar to Hayah Hoveh V'Yeheyeh.

Shaddai: General meaning is "that which is enough, that which suffices". Incorporates the conception that God as Creator and Sustainer is providing and moderating just the right amount of energy for the world as we know it to exist.

THE THIRTEEN ATTRIBUTES OF MERCY OF GOD – EXODUS 34:6,7:

There are many extraordinary stories and events in the Torah, some of them well known, and some of them not as well known. This relates to one of the lesser known stories. After the incident concerning the Golden Calf in the Wilderness after the Exodus, Moses went back up Mt. Sinai not only to receive the second set of Ten Commandments, but also to seek God's mercy to atone for his people for the horrible transgression that had just occurred. In an extraordinary and powerful colloquy between God and Moses, Moses beseeches God to provide Moses with a direct vision of His glory. God responds that no person can survive a direct vision of the essence of God, that the closest a person can come is to behold what follows from his existence. God places Moses in a crevice in the mountainside, and shields Moses from view as God passes by, lifting the shield after He has passed. As He passes, though, God proclaims what has become designated as His Thirteen Attributes of Mercy:

"The Lord, merciful and gracious God, long-suffering and abundant in mercy and truth; keeping mercy unto the thousandth generation, forgiving iniquity and transgression and sin, but Who will by no means clear the guilty; visiting iniquity of the fathers upon the children, and upon the children's children, unto the third and to the fourth generation."

Although there is some disagreement, following are the widely-accepted operative transliterated Hebrew words comprising these attributes, for which there are many different translations and much commentary on the various nuances of their meanings (YHVH is listed twice, as comprising two distinct types of mercy:

1.   YHVH (Tetragrammaton)

2.   YHVH (Tetragrammaton)

3.   El, Ale

4.   Rahchoom

5.   Chahnoon

6.   Ehrech Ahpahyeem

7.   Rahv-Chesed

8.   Rahv-Ehmet

9.   Notzair Chesed Lah ahlahfeem

10.   Nosay Ah ohz

11.   Nosay Fehshah

12.   Nosay Chahtah ah

13.   Nahkay

There is an event in Kings that is remarkable in its similarity to Moses' encounter above, in its equally powerful and poetic imagery, and in its substance. The prophet Elijah flees to the desert to escape from powerful enemies who want to kill him for prophesizing the truth. He believes his time has come, his mission has failed and is over, and he beseeches God to let him die in peace in the desert. Instead, as he sleeps, food and water miraculously appear, and he is awakened by an angel to partake of this sustenance. He continues to be sustained, and is directed to travel for 40 days and nights until he reaches Mt. Horeb, where he finds a cave in which he communes with God. God then instructs him to go to the mouth of the cave, and similar to Moses' experience, God passes before him. This time, accompanying God's passing is a great tumult of wind, rocks crashing and breaking, earthquakes and fire, but God was not in the wind, the earthquake or the fire; after all of the tumult died down, there came "a still small voice".

Chapter Eight

Jewish Yoga Meditation – A Primer
Other Hebrew Mantras

Jewish Yoga Meditation – A Primer

I do not pretend to be an expert on Jewish meditation, but I have been a practitioner and teacher of yoga meditation for many years. I have read some books on Jewish meditation and I have heard knowledgeable people speak on the subject. I have conducted some experimentation, based upon this background and experience. Although the proponents of Jewish meditation try to distinguish it from other forms, I see more similarities than differences. Through revelation and experimentation, I have discovered some powerful techniques that appear to have definite positive effects without any deleterious side effects. As in certain types of yoga meditation, these are practices that can be started without specific initiation from an external teacher. I do not know if there are other more advanced practices in Jewish meditation requiring the kind of initiation by a teacher described in the yoga tradition, although I suspect there are. Despite all of the continuing literature and exposure on Jewish mysticism, it still remains rather vague and shrouded in secrecy, particularly concerning the specifics of practices.

As in the yoga practices, one of these techniques involves coordination with the breath, and the other does not, instead involving rapid repetition of a phrase, called a "mantra" in yoga practice. I am not contending that these practices are only beneficial to Jewish people. As Judaism is the grandparent religion lying at the foundation of the other Western traditions that followed, I believe that these practices may have benefit for anyone, particularly in the Western world. Try them out and see for yourself!

GENERAL PROCEDURES APPLICABLE TO ALL OF THE PRACTICES

Although there may be forms of meditation involving externalized vocalizations and chanting, the general approach for these techniques is that they are to be performed internally, with external silence. It is preferable to do them with the eyes closed, but you can try it with the eyes opened also, and see the difference. The body should be in an upright seated position with the head, neck and trunk aligned. Breathing should be only through the nostrils, with the lips gently sealed. Breathing should be at a comfortable and natural pace, allowing the bodily intelligence and needs to set the rhythm, and it should be done diaphragmatically (abdomen gently rising during inhalation, and gently contracting during exhalation). There should be no extended pauses between inhalation and exhalation, just a natural continuous flow with that split second of suspension as it transitions from inhalation to exhalation, like the waves of the ocean coming onto the beach, turning, receding out, then turning and coming in again. There should also be a sense with the inhalation that your body is like an empty glass being filled with the breath, first pouring down to the bottom and filling it up as it goes. Likewise, with exhalation, the glass is emptied first from the top (being pushed up and out from the bottom), with the last bit of exhalation coming from the bottom. There should also be a sense of a circuit of energy flowing into the body and up the spine during inhalation, and flowing out and down the front of the body during exhalation, creating a circuit running up the spine and out through the nose and down the front of the body, then up the spine again, and so on.

Recommended time: 20 to 30 minutes, twice a day, on an empty stomach; best first thing in the morning, and either late afternoon before supper, or before bed-time.

THE BREATH COORDINATED PRACTICE
Background

In yoga, there is a traditional breath coordinated practice utilizing the "universal mantra" of "so-ham". I have discovered a similar Jewish practice employing the mysterious Tetragrammaton, YHVH, in conjunction with the likewise mysterious word "Elohim". Some discussion about these words is helpful to better understand and convey the power inherent in this practice. They are the two words most used in the Torah to refer to God. There are others as well, such as Adonoi, but these two are probably used the most. Sometimes one or the other is used, and sometimes they are used in conjunction. "Elohim" is the first word used in the Torah to refer to God, and is generally considered to encompass the Divine aspects of Judgement/ Severity/ Restriction/ Containment. Elohim was the Creator in Genesis because creation involved taking pure, unharnessed force and energy, and giving it form. YHVH follows later as a principle of flexibility/temperance/ mercy, so that the forms initiated by Elohim would not become too rigid or static. Without Elohim, we and the manifest world would never come into being; without YHVH, we and this manifest world would never survive for long. These two words and their accompanying principles also are reflected in the Kabala's Tree Of

Life/Jacob's Ladder, with YHVH/Mercy the right pillar, Elohim/Severity the left pillar, and their interaction the middle pillar, the middle way. Their interaction creates the rungs/paths along the middle way which allow ascent up the ladder. There are many other significant meanings and applications concerning these two words and their letters, but this will suffice for our purposes for now. The whole idea behind meditation is to employ it so that you will discover other layers and meanings.

YHVH is an English alphabetical transliteration of the Biblical Hebrew consonants with the same corresponding sounds, Yod (usually pronounced more like "Yud"), Heh (pronounced "Hay"), Vav, Heh. The Biblical Hebrew text of the Torah does not contain vowels, which were developed sometime later as little symbols above and below the consonants, utilized in other written documents. So even the written Torah, along with the purely oral Torah, was partly oral: the consonants served as mnemonic devices to remind one of the sound of the words with the vowels. The particular mystery behind YHVH, unlike other Biblical words, even Elohim, is that the correct pronunciation either is not known, or it is a mystery to be revealed only to high level initiates or priests. The vowels are not included in the texts that otherwise depict vowels for all other words. One common conception is that the correct pronunciation and intonation of this word is so powerful that mere unprepared mortals could not survive its power. An additional/alternative conception is that it is too pure and holy to be intoned by mere unprepared mortals, and doing so would inevitably lead to God's name being taken in vain. Thus its common description as the "ineffable" name. My intuitive insight is that its meaning, usage and value is so simple and subtle that unless one is properly prepared through preliminary study and practice, its real worth and value will not be grasped, appreciated and put to proper good use. I believe that this was one of the bases for much of the secrecy surrounding mystical practices in many traditions. Yes, perhaps they would be abused and could be dangerous in the wrong hands, but also, their profundity and simplicity would not be properly understood, valued or put to good and proper use unless the student was adequately trained and prepared. YHVH, by the way, is the source of references to the Jewish God "Yahweh" or "Yahveh" and "Jehovah".

One interpretation I discovered, which I have incorporated into this meditation practice, is that there are no secret vowels or correct pronunciation for the word YHVH, because the word, properly employed, is used in coordination with the breath. The sounds of the consonants are intoned in coordination with the breath, and the sounds of the vowels are the sound of the breath itself. Basically, the sound of this word is the sound of the breath, which is the same conception as with the "So-ham" mantra in the yoga tradition.

Layer One Practice

(Note: for the basic revelation related to this practice, I am deeply indebted to Reb Zalman Schacter-Shalomi, Rabbi Arthur Waskow, and Rabbi Phyllis Berman).

The first layer of practice in this meditation is done as follows. Each Heh is silently intoned within in coordination with the inhalation and the exhalation. The Yod is silently intoned at the moment transitioning from exhalation to inhalation, and the Vav is silently intoned at the moment transitioning from inhalation to exhalation. Thus, right before the beginning of the inbreath is Yod transitioning to Heh for the duration of the inbreath, then Vav is intoned just as the inbreath has completed and is turning to the outbreath, sliding into the second Heh for the duration of the outbreath. I have found it most comfortable to intone the sound of the full name of each letter instead of just the beginning sound, in other words "Yod" instead of "Yeh", "Vav" instead of "Veh", "Hay" instead of "Huh". I hope you get what I mean. I would suggest you experiment with this to see what feels right to you. Maybe just the pure sound of the letter, and not the sound of its name, feels better for you.

Layer Two Practice

If the first layer gets a little boring after a while and is not sufficient to quiet and preoccupy "the monkey mind", there are second and third layers which should help to quiet and focus the chatter. For the reasons stated above under "Background", these layers incorporate the word "Elohim" into the practice. This is not a mere clever, inventive concoction, but is based upon scriptural support. At a key juncture in the development of Abram, at Genesis 15:2, he intones the first appearance in the Torah of the word "Adonoi", used in conjunction with YHVH/Elohim, but in a most unusual manner, as explained by the notes in the Stone Edition. First of all, it is unusual to use Adonoi in conjunction with YHVH or Elohim. Secondly, although YHVH and Elohim are often used in conjunction, with one word following the other (usually YHVH goes first), in this rare, fascinating, and extremely significant instance, although the consonants of YHVH are used in the main text alone, not followed by the consonants for the word Elohim, the notes state that the oral tradition has designated that it is to be coordinated with the vowels for Elohim and pronounced as Elohim. This appears to be the only occurrence of this formulation in the Torah, although the notes indicate a few places in Psalms where it is utilized. It came to me that a viable alternative is that both words are meant to be pronounced simultaneously, reflecting/resonating the true interaction of these two words and their accompanying principles/energies, merging into a third word, if you will, representative of the dynamically balanced energy of the middle pillar itself. As traditional proponents of Jewish meditation have pointed out, Abram/Abraham, considered to be the first Jew, is also considered to be the master, if not the originator, of meditation and related mystical powers. Abram first addresses God here at this juncture in the Torah, utilizing/intoning these holy names. This would most likely be accomplished through a meditative process.

The layer two practice incorporates this notion of simultaneously intoning both words. After the layer one practice is established, in addition to the intonations of the layer one practice, simultaneously add the intonation of the sound, "El" on inhalation and "ohim" (pronounced "oheem") on exhalation. This can be done, and it is interesting to note the added focus required of the mind to maintain it, and how the mind shifts foreground and background between the two sets of sounds. In other words, you are silently intoning within "El" at the same time as Yod-Heh, and "Ohim" at the same time as Vav-Heh.

Layer Three Practice

After the layer two practice is established, in addition to those two simultaneous sets of intonations, add yet a third layer: intone the entire word, "Elohim" with inhalation alone and again with exhalation alone. Practicing at this level will definitely keep the monkey mind well occupied, and you just might find that the monkey mind gets so tired from this hard work, that it falls asleep in exhaustion, thus opening the door to what is referred to in yoga meditation as "the unstruck sound", the inner paradoxical sound current of silence. Thus the path to a deeper level of meditation.

I hope this description is clear enough to convey the technique so that it can be practiced. In summation, when practicing all three levels at once, with inhalation and exhalation, three sounds are intoned simultaneously (remember, at layer one, Yod is very brief and slides into Heh, and Vav is likewise very brief and slides into the second Heh):

Inhalation/Yod-Heh/El/Elohim
Exhalation/Vav-Heh/Ohim/Elohim

You can also experiment with trying each layer separately.

THE REPETITIVE PHRASE PRACTICE
Background

In yoga and other meditative traditions, there is a common practice of repeating particular phrases/mantras in a fast repetitive fashion not coordinated with the breath. Some of these mantras have a "rounding" effect, in that the ending sound of the phrase is the same as or similar to the beginning sound, so that they blend into each other, aiding in a sense of a seamless continuity in the practice. An example of this is the common eastern phrase, "Om Mani Padme Hum", in which the ending "Hum" blends into the beginning "Om". I have discovered such phrasing in one version of the most central of all Jewish prayers, the "Shema". I am not a big fan of transliteration, but for the sake of those readers not familiar with Hebrew and Jewish prayers, I will give it a shot. I would encourage you to review your pronunciation with someone familiar with Hebrew and this prayer:

> *Shema Yisrael Adonoi Elohanu Adonoi Echad*
> *Echad Elohanu Gadol Adonanu Kadosh Shemo*

The general meaning of the single words, without a lot of layered explication:

The first sentence:

Shema: Hear (not just surface hearing, but deep inner hearing)

Yisrael: Israel (there are many layers of meaning to this word/concept)

Adonoi: Chapter 7 contains a discussion of the meaning and significance of this word in its own right, and how it is also used as a substitute pronunciation in prayers where the unpronounceable Tetragrammaton, YHVH, is designated. In the Shema prayer, YHVH is designated, but is pronounced "Adonoi". It is usually translated as "Lord".

Elohanu: A possessive derivative of Elohim. What is interesting about Elohim is that it is the plural form, where Elohanu is the singular form. Elohim is the creator in Genesis.

Adonoi: YHVH is again designated here. See above.

Echad: One. This prayer is conveying the central message of Judaism that there is one God, one unifying, underlying source for all manifest and unmanifest existence.

So the first sentence, literally translated:

> *Hear Israel Lord Our Creator Lord One*

The second sentence:

Echad: One. This prayer is conveying the central message of Judaism that there is one God, one unifying, underlying source for all manifest and unmanifest existence.

Elohanu: A possessive derivative of Elohim. What is interesting about Elohim is that it is the plural form, where Elohanu is the singular form. Elohim is the creator in Genesis.

Gadol: Big, Vast, Great

Adonanu: A possessive derivative of Adonoi, here used as a word in its own right, and not as a substitute pronunciation for YHVH. It was first used by Abram in addressing God, as distinguished from Elohim and YHVH, which are God's own self references.

Kadosh: Holy

Shemo: Name

The second sentence, literally translated:

One Our Creator Great Our Lord Holy Name

Literal summary:

Shema Yisrael Adonoi Elohanu Adonoi Echad
Echad Elohanu Gadol Adonanu Kadosh Shemo

Hear Israel Lord Our Creator Lord One
One Our Creator Great Our Lord Holy Name

A common prayer book translation, rendering it grammatically correct:

Hear, O Israel, the Lord our God, the Lord is One.
One is our God, great is our Lord, holy is His name.

Again, there are many layers of meaning to everything, but I'll repeat here the most wondrous mystical meaning I have discovered, from *God is a Verb, Kabbalah and the Practice of Mystical Judaism,* by Rabbi David A. Cooper:

"The mystery of saying the Shema prayer is that it draws a beam of light from a hidden supernal world and divides it into seventy lights, representing the seventy nations of creation. Those lights become luminous branches of the Tree of Life. When the seventy branches are illuminated, this tree and all other trees in the Garden of Eden emit sweet odors and perfumes, preparing all the polarities to unite into the Divine Oneness. In Kabbalah, the urge for this union, bringing the upper and lower together, is the driving force of the process of creation, the process of our lives." (p 51)

"Israel is a code word for that essence in life that longs to be with its Creator. The word "Israel" is composed of two words: Yashar and El. Yashar means "to go straight," and El is one of the names of God. The aspect within every being which yearns to go straight to God is called Israel. Each person

knows the part of themselves that desires to be with God. This is the mystical meaning of the nation of Israel; it is not a geographical location, for it extends throughout the universe." (p 319, fn 70)

The traditional explanation of Israel: "He who has struggled with the divine and with men, and has prevailed". This is the name and its meaning given to Jacob by the angel with whom he wrestled all night. He would not let the angel go until the angel blessed him, and the blessing was to bestow upon Jacob the name "Israel". It has come to signify the inner struggle we all have, trying to balance our sometimes discordant impulses, particularly in our attempts to reconcile our animal impulses with our Divine impulse.

<u>The Practice</u>

Now for the practice: These phrases are to be said in rapid silent repetition, with the "Echad" at the end of the first phrase blurring into the "Echad" at the beginning of the second phrase, so that there is only one "Echad". Likewise, the "Shemo" at the end of the second phrase should blend with the "Shema" at the beginning of the first phrase, so that there is only one "Shemo/Shema". I have been using one traditional yoga mala of 108 repetitions followed by silent sitting. In Judaism, the number 18, signifying the numerical value of the word "Chai", which means "life" is an important number, often used by itself or in multiples, and as you see, 108 is a multiple of 6 times 18. You might want to experiment with different multiples of 18. I have found this to be a very powerful, grounding and centering practice, again leading to a deeper level of inner silence.

As with the other meditation practice, it should be done sitting upright comfortably with the head, neck and trunk aligned, employing diaphragmatic breathing with the mouth closed (abdomen gently expanding on inhalation, and contracting on exhalation), on an empty stomach, for 20 to 30 minutes at a time, twice a day (first thing in the morning, and either late afternoon before supper, or late evening before retiring). Again, eyes closed is preferable to tap into deeper inner realms, but it may be worthwhile experimenting with eyes open.

In yoga, the process of rapid repetition of a mantra like this is called "japa", which can then become what is called "ajapa japa", where it takes on its own momentum and just goes by itself, and you're just listening to it. If it becomes an imperceptible drone, so be it. It may be meant to become an imperceptible drone, as are a lot of mantras when they get to a deeper level, approaching the source of all sound. That is the idea behind all meditation that utilizes intonation of a phrase. The conception is that those sounds actually already exist within you. On an outer level, you are intoning those sounds to make the connection. Once the connection is made to this inner level of sound that already exists, intonation can cease, and listening can begin. If you can get to the point where you're just listening, you just listen. You can get to a point where the listening phase comes fairly quickly and easily. There is also a process akin to shifting layers; you go to different layers and hear different things at the different layers, analogous to changing the station on a radio. It is just a subtle shifting. You can fine tune inside and go to different layers and hear different sounds. Sometimes the sounds come and are asking for your attention. If a sound comes and is asking for your attention, it would probably be advisable to listen to it. If anything else comes asking for your attention that is a pleasant, joyful kind of experience, whatever inner sense it may involve, pay attention to it. There are inner spiritual sensations of sight, sound, touch, taste and smell that parallel our outer five senses. If it is not pleasant, ignore it, or note it for what it is, and then let it go. I think the pleasant ones are there for us to enjoy and to help us develop, so we shouldn't be afraid or threatened by them if we can open up to them. If there is something very emotionally charged, negative, unpleasant, that's what you want to note and then let go and find "your happy place". The pleasant experiences involve finding our internal "happy places". These are very potent happy places and not just our imaginings of laying on the beach or something like that. There is something inside that is asking for your attention.

One repetition of the Shema is traditionally said by Jews upon retiring at night and upon rising in the morning, as there is language in the Torah that has been seen as a dictate to this effect. My suggestion is to experiment with these two practices as AM and PM practices, using them in the same session, or perhaps using one in the AM and the other in the PM, and see what feels right for you. The rapid repetition practice may be better in the AM, as its seems more invigorating, for a start to the day, and the Breath-coordinated practice better in the PM, as it seems more sedative, as a wind-down to the day.

Other Hebrew Mantras

Concerning Hebrew mantras, as far as authenticity goes, that is a tricky question. I have never heard of any reference to an authentic, authoritative source or text that specifically identifies Hebrew mantras and provides instructions on how to utilize them. I believe this was always left for direct oral instruction and transmission, and self-discovery and experimentation. Most of the Jewish Meditation teachers with whom I have studied and techniques that I have read about are fairly consistent in their basic approach. They use various prayers or phrases from traditional Jewish liturgy or sources, especially prayers or phrases that originated in the Torah, and employ them with methods similar to how yoga utilizes mantras.

In addition to the two-lined Shema prayer discussed earlier in this chapter, what many people don't realize is that the Shema prayer technically includes not only these one or two lines, but three other paragraphs that follow it. The first paragraph is certainly the most well-known, beginning with the phrase referenced by Jesus when asked to summarize the most important of the commandments, that you should "love God will all thy heart, with all thy soul, and with all thy mind/might". The other most central prayer in Judaism is known as the Shimoneh Esray (meaning "The Eighteen", as there were originally 18 blessings in it, although a 19th controversial one was added later), also called The Amida, which means "The Standing", as you are to recite it standing up. My interpretation is that it is to be recited with the body erect without the aid of supports, with head, neck and trunk aligned and perpendicular to the ground, as in a seated meditation posture, and not necessarily as standing up on your feet. The entire Amida is not verbatim from the Torah, as is the case with the Shema, but it does incorporate phrases from the Torah, including the well-known "priestly blessing". Another interesting aspect to the Amida from a meditation perspective is that although it is an important part of the congregational prayer service, it is the one part of the service said individually in silence. I include the Shema, its first paragraph, and an abbreviated form of the Amida in my daily Jewish Yoga meditation practice, all internally in silence.

There is a tradition in Judaism called "Midrash", which allows for students and scholars with insights to place their own spins and interpretations on the main authoritative texts. These midrash, affirmed and repeated over time, then become recognized as their own authority. The Zohar, one of the principle Kabbalistic texts, is actually in the form of a midrash/commentary on the Torah, although its author is still disputed (it is narrowed down to one of two people by most scholars). The Bahir and Sefer Yetzirah are two of the other principle Kabbalistic texts, and no-one is certain of their authorship. An argument among some quarters is being made that the process of midrash must remain alive with current practitioners in order for the tradition to remain alive, dynamic and vital, and as such, anyone can create midrash. This may bring authenticity into question, but I think it is vital that current students, even this writer, be allowed to voice our own insights and revelations. One of the criticisms of Jewish scholarship over the centuries is that many of the midrash were more intellectual gymnastics/sophistry rather than expressing any real experiential insights. The practices I describe originate in authentic tradition, but then are extrapolated from those traditions, both Jewish and yogic, tweaking certain practices. They are based not on my intellectual imaginings, but rather on intuitive and experiential insights and practices. So you can see why I say that authenticity is a tricky question.

For anyone interested in Jewish Meditation and utilizing Hebrew mantras in their meditation practice, I suggest that you experiment with some of the practices described in this and the next chapter. Then study a traditional Jewish prayer book and the Jewish Bible for prayers, blessings or phrases that particularly resonate with you, and try using them as mantras, with and without breath-coordination. Besides the Five Books of Moses (the Torah proper), phrases from Psalms and the Song of Songs have been of particular inspiration to many people.

Although it is a favored practice of mine, as described in the breath-coordinated section, I know that there are issues about utilizing the Tetragrammaton or approximations of it in any way, as there are long-held traditions and beliefs that either the correct pronunciation is no longer known, and even if known, should not be spoken or even thought because it would be using the name of the Lord in vain. My childhood rabbi, who was Modern Orthodox and pretty straight-laced, told me that the correct pronunciation is known, but is just a well-kept secret for advanced students only. The Jewish Renewal take, as described earlier in this chapter, is that it can't really be "spoken" out loud or even internally as a word, because it really isn't a word in the common sense and doesn't have vowels, because it is the sound of the breath. You could also say it is the Word as described in the gospel of John, which is of course, like all early "Christian" writings, based upon Jewish belief and practice: "In the beginning was the Word, and the Word was with God, and the Word was God." The idea is just to internally intone/coordinate the approximation of the sound of YH on inhalation and VH on exhalation, and really to then just let the breath do the work. One of my favorite quotes of my yoga meditation mentor, Swami Rama, from his book "The Art of Joyful Living", is a rare section where he actually talks about his practice. He says he doesn't mess around with all of the preliminaries he teaches his students. He just gets right into turning his inner being into an internal "ear" by which he listens to his mantra, which is already there of its own accord. So he really isn't "doing" his mantra, he is just listening to it, as it has an internal life of its own. This is what in yoga is called "ajapa japa", whereby the rapid repetition is not initiated or maintained by any effort of the practitioner. Rather, it takes on a life of its own, whereby the practitioner is placed more in the role of a listener/receiver. This is consistent with Jewish teachings as the term "Kabala" comes from the root word meaning "to receive", and "Shema" means "Hear". The beauty of these breath-coordinated practices are that they are aligning their sounds with the breath, and letting the breath become the sounds of its own accord. So you could say that this practice is not "speaking" or even "thinking" the word, either externally or internally, not even as a thought. It is something beyond and deeper than thought. It is alignment with life force and its source.

Consonants do have sounds even without formal vowels accompanying them: Y = Yeh or Yuh; H = Heh or Huh; V = Veh or Vah. Also, they can be sounded by the names of their letters Y = Yod or Yud; H = Heh; V = Vav or Vuv. My yoga tradition encourages exploration, so the whole idea is for the practitioner to go with the suggestion and experiment with it and see what feels right. Perhaps it is time to overcome and explore resistance due to childhood restrictions and taboos. All mantras ultimately lead to silence, but on the surface level there is sound, and it becomes more subtle as it is aligned with the breath and becomes the sound of the breath.

However, for those who remain uncomfortable employing anything related to the Tetragrammaton as a mantra, there are other biblical names/designations for God in the Jewish tradition that might be suitable, many of which have been previously discussed in Chapter 7. "Adonai" is the first name used by man/Abraham in addressing God. "El Shaddai" is another common potent designation, and also contains a feminine aspect, as it shares the same root as the word for "breast", suggesting nurturance. This is discussed in more detail in the next chapter. When Moses asked God whom should he say had sent him to the slaves in Egypt, God responded, "Tell them 'Ehyeh Asher Ehyeh' sent you", which is generally translated as "I Am That I Am". It also conveys the timeless connotation of simultaneously being "I was, I am, and I will be" designated by the similar phrase, "Hayah Hoveh V'ehyeh". Yet another simple designation that is currently in favor with the Jewish Renewal movement is the simple "Yah", meaning "I am". Other possibilities might include the Hebrew term for Israel, "Yisrael", "Baruch", "Atah", or any other of a number of blessings or prayers.

A female connotation roughly similar to Kundalini Shakti in the yoga tradition is "Shechinah" (a feminine noun with the accent on the second syllable). This is defined as the aspect of God's presence in the world. It was the Shechinah that communicated with Moses and the High Priests from the Ark. When the Torah speaks of creating a suitable place for God's presence to dwell among us, it is the Shechinah that is to be doing the dwelling. There is also the idea that a suitable "dwelling" for God's presence was not only meant to be the Ark and the Tabernacle, but rather the human body, as the human body is also designated as a Temple, and the actual Temple building is seen as a depiction/representation of the human body and vice-versa.

There is also a lesser-known designation for God steeped with mystical mystery which might be suitable for use as a mantra: "Emesh". According to Rabbi Aryeh Kaplan, an incredible modern (but unfortunately, deceased) mystical orthodox scholar, in his commentary on the Sefer Yetzirah, this word is composed of the three "Mother" letters of Aleph, Mem and Shin. It is used in the Torah and other

Jewish scripture, often translated as the dark gloom of night, suggestive of the time of deep dreamless sleep, of the deepest recesses of the unconscious. It represents all kinds of things, including a reference to the Ein/Ayin/Void underlying all of existence (similar to Brahman in the yoga tradition and shunyata in Buddhism), a reconciliation of opposites and the mystery to master fire.

During the event when Moses encounters the burning bush on Mt. Sinai, when the voice of God calls out to Moses, his response is, "Hinani" (phonetically, "Hee-Nay-Nee"). This is translated as "Here I am", or "I am here.", but the commentary on the inner meaning of this response is very significant. This is not the common separative "I/self" asserting itself and indicating physical location, but rather the humble vestige of a separative self responding in awe to the greatness of the Almighty which it is beholding, and offering up itself in complete submission and service. "I am at your service", would be a more correct translation capturing the inner meaning of the literal translation. As when Abraham earlier addressed God as "Adonai", here again is an utterance of another great servant of God in response to God's call. So I believe that "Hinani" would be another suitable term to use as a Hebrew mantra. I have utilized "Adonai Hinani" in conjunction and I have found it to be very powerful: internally intone "Adonai" on inhalation, breathing in the Divine essence offered by God; and "Hinani" on exhalation, extending back to God our offer of unconditional service. I highly recommend it as an alternative to the YHVH practice described earlier, or in addition to it.

And finally, in Chapter 7, I list the Thirteen Attributes of Mercy of God as found in Exodus 34:6,7 which were revealed by God to Moses during an extraordinary event on Mt. Sinai. One or more of them might also be appealing to some as Hebrew mantras.

***

FINAL NOTES

"And thou shall love the Lord thy God with all thine heart, and with all thy soul, and with all thy might. And these words, which I command thee this day, shall be upon thine heart: and thou shalt teach them diligently unto thy children, and shalt talk of them when thou sittest in thine house, and when thou walkest by the way, and when thou liest down, and when thou risest up. And thou shalt bind them for a sign upon thine hand, and they shall be for frontlets between thine eyes. And thou shalt write them upon the door posts of thy house, and upon thy gates." Deuteronomy 6:4-9, incorporated as the second paragraph to the full Shema prayer.

For those familiar with Eastern teachings, this is strikingly similar to the Eastern practice of always remembering God and always repeating His Name. Any of the practices described in this chapter can be taken with you during the day and utilized during spare moments to refresh yourself and reconnect. While standing on a line or waiting at a red light in a car or in gridlock, try a little breath awareness and meditation (with eyes open, as necessary, or eyes closed, if possible). You might find it very helpful, invigorating, and refreshing.

Chapter Nine

Jewish Healing Meditation:
Ruach El Shaddai – Breath of Balance

<u>Introduction</u>

There has been increasing focus over the years in various avenues for healing in addition to Western medicine. One avenue has been in the area of healing meditation practices, something for which I had somewhat shamefully never had much interest, as my general perspective had been that meditation in and of itself is a significant tool for healing oneself, and individuals healed through their own meditation practices will create a spill-over effect into their environment and in their interchanges with their fellow beings. However, out of curiosity, I attended an introductory presentation on "Pranic Healing" as formulated by the late Master Choa Kuk Sui, and decided to take the initial training. Attending this course impressed upon me the importance of more directly aiding the healing of others, and challenged me to ponder what kind of approach would feel most comfortable for me. As a result of these musings, a formulation for a Jewish Healing Meditation came to me that I first published on my blog, and which I am now presenting below. It is a synthesis of three main sources: it borrows and builds upon some of the principles I learned in the Pranic Healing Course, in conjunction with some tweaks to basic breathing, relaxation and stress management techniques I learned through my study of yoga, and further incorporates principles from the mystical Jewish tradition. In keeping with my own personal introverted pre-disposition towards internalized methods, intentional procedures and interventions, as such, are kept to a minimum and are all enacted silently within. While this may sound like a New Age mish-mash, I feel it is a very profound and effective technique founded in time-tested traditions, updated for our current circumstances whereby many elements of world spiritual healing cultures are melding, resulting in the emergence of new forms. I invite the reader to try it for themselves, approaching it with an open heart and mind, and come to their own conclusions.

The Theory

As is usually the case, there are many layers of meaning to these biblical Hebrew terms, "Ruach El Shaddai," but for the purpose of this practice, "Breath of Balance" is a simple and appropriate English translation. Comparable to the five layers of a being described in yoga, there are five levels of the soul enumerated in Jewish teachings. In the Jewish scheme, "ruach" is one level removed from the grossest level, nefesh. However, it is also the word utilized in Genesis designating the spirit/wind that hovered over the face of the deep at the beginning of creation. It is considered that when God breathed life into the nostrils of inanimate man, God was exhaling this "ruach", breath, life force, comparable to the second layer in the yoga system, called "prana". In yoga, "pranayama" is often translated as "breathing exercises", because it is maintained that the essential life force of prana rides with the breath, and through breathing practices, one is also regulating the flow of this more subtle life force. The practice of Ruach El Shaddai/Breath of Balance incorporates and builds upon basic yogic breathing/pranayama practices, so "breath" is an appropriate term, although one should keep in mind that it incorporates the concept of prana/life force/spirit.

While God the Creator is designated in Genesis as "Elohim", at other points in the Torah, "Shaddai" is one of a few other interesting significant designations of a particular quality/function of God. A common conception to "Shaddai" is that it expresses a quality to the Creator whereby just the right amount of energy in form, quality and quantity was utilized in order to bring about the multitude of the forms of creation. Associated with this is the idea of moderating energy to the extent of "that which suffices" to bring about the desired result; not too much, not too little, just right. There is a further elaboration to this quality that it applies not only to the initial creative function, but in keeping with the idea that "God is a Verb", it also applies to the ongoing Divine function that continues to create and sustain the universe in just the right proportions. These two functions just described correspond with the designations in yoga as God the Creator, Brahma and God the Sustainer/Maintainer, Vishnu. While it may not be as explicitly recognized as such in the Jewish tradition, the Torah is replete with stories depicting the third aspect in yoga of God the Destroyer/Dissolver, Shiva. It is clear in the Torah that creation is not static, but dynamic, and that old forms constantly need to be dismantled to give way to new forms.

Another interesting aspect to the term "Shaddai" is that it shares the same root as the term for "breast" and thus carries with it the connotation of perfect nurturance, obviously also associated with breasts and female energy. "Shaddai" translated as "balance" is meant to incorporate the ideas that this quality of

Shaddai contains these aspects of perfect nurturing that provides and maintains balance (that which suffices), but it is a *dynamic*, not a *static*, balance.

It is this "Breath of Balance" and the three associated functions described above that we are seeking to invoke in our healing sessions to restore balance where there is imbalance, in keeping with the kabalistic conception that our goal is to ascend the middle balanced pillar on the Tree of Life. We are not "doing" the healing, we are merely invoking the Divine healing powers that exist to assist our subjects through the agency of our focused intent. Our intervention and manipulation is thus minimal, as is the possibility for any mistakes, as we are invoking powers and energies beyond us that work in perfect harmony and balance. We systematically invoke first the cleansing Dissolver aspect, to rid our subjects of the negative "dirty energy" and obstructions that are causing their imbalance; second, we invoke the rejuvenating Creator aspect to restore regenerative nurturing energy to heal our subjects; and last, we invoke the stabilizing Sustainer/Maintainer aspect to circulate, assimilate and maintain the renewed energy in our subjects.

The magic and effectiveness of this healing lies in the words, "focus", "invoke" and "intent". We have been imbued with these gifts of being able to use our mind as an instrument of our individual consciousness connected to universal consciousness, to focus our attention and intent, and invoke powers that lie beyond our mortal limitations.

Any kind of healing can be addressed, whether it be physical, mental or a combination. Positive qualities (virtues) can be nurtured while their negative opposites (vices) can be minimized. There is no need for the subject to be present or in close proximity or even aware of your efforts, although it may magnify the effect if the subject is made aware and thus can open up receptivity on their part, even to the extent of participating at the same time, if not the same place. While there may be a benefit to physical proximity and coordination of time (the healing session occurring at the same time that the subject is aware and receptive to it, and even following along in participation), we are working at a level where proximity and simultaneity and cooperation are not essential, although helpful. Time and space are receding and being transcended, and after all, the subject is present with us all of the time on the planet earth.

The Practice

1. **Preliminary stage.** This can be performed lying down or sitting up, with the head, neck and trunk in a straight line. Begin with normal yoga breathing and relaxation, using diaphragmatic breathing and breathing only through the

nostrils. For those familiar, this can be followed by normal yoga meditation or Jewish Yoga meditation if in the seated posture.

2. **Focus on the subject of the healing.** After the preliminary stage has been established, bring the attention to the subject of the healing. It is advisable to always begin with oneself as the first subject, as there is usually some need to heal some aspect of oneself, and after healing oneself, you will be better equipped to focus your healing efforts on other subjects. Proceed with the following steps in a complete sequential set for each chosen subject. In other words, do all of the steps in sequence for a selected subject, then begin the process over again for the next subject. It is recommended to end the session with the planet earth as the subject, as there is always need to assist our planet as a whole to heal and attain dynamic balance. The focus on the subject can be narrowed to a specific ailment or group of ailments, or just to the general energy level of the subject. There is no need for the subject to be present or in close proximity or even aware of your efforts, although it may be helpful if the subject is made aware and thus can open up receptivity on their part. We are working at a level where proximity, cooperation, participation, receptivity is helpful, but not essential, as time and space recede and are transcended, and after all, the subject is present with us all of the time on the planet earth.

3. **Elimination of "dirty" energy causing imbalance through focus on exhalation.** While maintaining attention on the subject and any specific condition or group of conditions, focus first on the exhalation, regarding the inhalation, which automatically occurs, as just a reloading and preparation for the next exhalation. With each exhalation, visualize all forms of "dirty energy" (negative energy/vibrations, influences, obstructions, depletions, congestions, weaknesses, stresses) that are the cause of the imbalance in the subject being released and flowing out of the subject. Being invoked by your intent and channeled by your exhalation, visualize the Great Force of Destruction/Disintegration/Dissolution removing all of this "dirty energy" in a gentle manner which will not be harmful or shocking to the subject. Dissolve it in the vastness of the cosmos, which is capable of absorbing and recycling everything. If it is helpful, visualize a great Fire or Sun either suspended in the air, on the ground, on a sacrificial altar, or whatever image feels comfortable to you, and visualize that your exhalation is assisting to channel all of this dirty energy out of the subject and into that Fire or Sun for dissolution. Retain the focus with each exhalation simultaneously on the subject, any specified

ailments, and the dirty energy flowing out of the subject and being dissolved. Continue this focus on exhalation/elimination/dissolution until you feel it is sufficient for now.

4. **Introduction of healing energy to aid in the restoration of balance through focus on inhalation.** Keeping the subject and specific condition in focus, now shift the focus to the inhalation, regarding the exhalation, which automatically occurs, as just a reloading and preparation for the next inhalation. With each inhalation, visualize all forms of "healing energy" (regeneration, rejuvenation, positive energy/good vibrations, nurturance, health, relaxation) that can relieve and cure the distressed condition and restore balance flowing into the subject. Being invoked by your intent and guided by your inhalation, visualize the infinite resource of the Great Force of Creation/Nurturance providing exactly the precise form, quality and quantity of healing energy needed to effectuate the healing process in a gentle manner which will not be harmful or shocking to the subject. If it is helpful, as before, visualize a great inexhaustible Fire or Sun from which is emanating this healing energy in the needed form, quality and quantity, which your inhalation is assisting to channel to the subject for their benefit. Retain the focus with each inhalation simultaneously on the subject, any specified ailments, and the healing energy flowing into the subject to restore balance. Continue this focus on inhalation/rejuvenation/nurturance until you feel it is sufficient for now.

5. **Stabilize the newly introduced healing energy through focusing equally on inhalation and exhalation.** Now shift the focus to the subject as a self-enclosed entity. Focus equally on inhalation and exhalation which is creating a cycle/circuit of flowing energy within the subject. Being invoked by your intent and guided by your focus on this cycle of inhalation and exhalation, visualize the Great Force of Sustaining/Maintaining providing exactly what is needed to seal off the channels through which the dirty energy was earlier eliminated and through which the healing energy was earlier introduced. Circulate the newly acquired healing energy throughout the subject in a gentle manner which is not harmful or shocking. It will effectuate the greatest benefit for the subject by acting to stabilize this new healing energy and allowing it to be properly assimilated. Continue this focus equally on a circuit of inhalation and exhalation until you feel it is sufficient for now. The healing session for this subject is now complete.

6. **Repeat with the next subject.** If you have chosen more than one subject, continue with the other subjects, repeating steps 2 through 5 for each subject in succession. Conclude with the planet earth as a whole for the final subject. Meditation can then continue, or the session can be brought to an end in the same gentle manner you would bring any meditation session to an end.

Om Shalom.

Chapter Ten

THE SILENCE

There is the Silence. The throbbing, dynamic Silence. It is the seed state, the potential from which all things manifest. It is the Ground of existence. If you have ever sensed a silence, a momentary peace, a rest, you have sensed this Silence. Listen closely, and you will see that it is always present, never-changing, without form. It is thrilling. Amidst decibels of noise and confusion it can be sensed and felt. Know it just for a fleeting moment, and know some peace. Know it always, and know eternal peace. It never leaves. Your awareness may lose it, but it never leaves. Do not belittle its significance. It is peace. It is a fathomless source of strength and creativity. It is the Ground. Have you ever sensed some silence? That silence is the source of unbounded happiness and the springboard for all the temporary and ever-changing manifestations of energy that we call life. It is never-changing and without form. It is silence. Just silence, nothing more. Realize this Silence that permeates the universe, that is the very medium through which everything moves, that underlies all being, and your life will become full, your death empty and without fear. You may lose touch with it, but it is always here. Establish this awareness and you will be happy. It is that simple. Stop standing in the way with gross resistance and become transparent. Realize the medium you are moving through. Feel it. It is the Ground. It is vibrant, brim full with the presence of life. It is not life, it is not death. It is peace. It is Silence. It is that simple. And it is screaming in your ear.

The awareness of what was just said is all that is necessary for total happiness and knowledge of the universe to unfold before you like a magnificent gift being unwrapped before a baby. It cannot be made much simpler or clearer. All that follows is elaboration.

*   *   *

It is up to you. Can't you hear the Silence? Feel it? Sense it? It is consoling, it is cold, yet comforting. It is absolute zero. It is exhilarating. We add the warmth and the life. The joy and the ecstasy; the pain and the suffering too. This is creation. These are our creations. Revel in them. Completely. Know the cold haughty silence from which they arise and you will love every minute of it. An uncontrollable bellylaugh, a snicker, a sneer. The endless rise and fall of push-pull, action-reaction; creation. Know this and know Sanity. Know this and know Insanity. The Paradox. Beware!

*   *   *

Engage your awareness with Silence and your energy with life. When you lose it and you realize you have lost it, engage it again. And again. Eventually it will lock into place and you won't need to engage it. You will be engaged, and shake your head in disbelief at how simple it actually is. It will remain. The Silence remains. Doubt and insecurity become fleeting luxuries that only gain life through the entertainment of an idle mind. Engage in creation, engage in silence and there will be little room for the shallow ghosts of doubt and fear. Walk the razor's edge that keeps you safe from icy despair and be comfortable. This is the power and the strength of a glistening warrior shaking in his boots with fear. It is not complicated. It is awesome and empty. Why go on any other way?

*   *   *

Deity is a concept of the mind, emotion and psyche. It is a manifestation of energy through which we often find it necessary to relate. At best, it is a channel to the void, the Silence. At worst, it serves to confuse. Silence lies before the mind, before emotion, before psyche. And before Deity. It lies after them, too. And at all points in between. Deity as a concept of energy is unnecessary. Or at least it becomes unnecessary. Lay it down and discover the Silence, traditionally known as the Father. Pick it up and discover creation, traditionally known as the Mother. Do not get hung up on elaboration.

*   *   *

A good teacher serves only as a catalyst and insists that the student stand on his own two feet. A good teacher does not want disciples or praise. Gurus, holy men, esteemed teachers and the like thrive on the existence of disciples. The disciples must destroy the guru-function; make it obsolete through its disuse if they are ever to be truly happy. A good teacher does not want students as followers. A good teacher pushes students away so they will stand alone together. He wants friends and companions of mutual respect, not fawning sheep. He wants equals, not subordinates. He wishes to share the burden of his aloneness. The Guru must cease to function, to wither away through disuse and die. Then there

130

will be the Dawn. Take your life in your hands and realize it is not yours or anyone's. This is the Dawn.

A good teacher does not demand or expect unusual gifts or support. A good teacher supports himself. Support yourself. Respect yourself. Respect others. Offer others their dignity whether they respect themselves or not. They will take what they can whether they seem grateful or not. This is the Dawn.

*   *   *

There are but a few things to be sure of: There is the Silence, the immutable. Of this you can be certain; you can be certain of no-thing. This alone can give you peace. There is a never-ending formulation and re-formulation of energy; all is valid with no right or wrong. You can be certain of anything and everything. This alone can breed frustration and confusion, but can serve as a crisis to point towards peace. There is the Heart; the source of the purest human motivation and mode of perception – the source of Love. It is the human organ that connects the manifest with the unmanifest, constantly burning and purifying, providing for wholesome, clean and simple living. Re-turn to the Silence, sacrifice to the Heart, and engage Life. You will never stray far from contentment, happiness, and lust.

*   *   *

Silence is not merely the absence of anything or everything. Silence is no-thing; it is a Presence. It is what is inside an empty bell-jar. Put an object in the bell-jar and no-thing is still there, along with something. Take that object away, and no-thing remains. Something is gone; but no-thing remains. This is not a quaint play on words. No-thing is always present. Do no-thing. Get out of the way. Feel the heat of resistance and finally dissolve. You do nothing but let it happen.

*   *   *

Perhaps you are holding back, like a tentative lover, savoring in the delicacy of the situation, the last few moments of hesitation and fear, knowing full well that you are about to be overwhelmed. Be overwhelmed already. Give in and let go. All that hurts is fear and resistance.

Perhaps you are like the over-anxious lover, too eager to plunge in and force the Dance. You will be left quickly spent and unsatisfied. It cannot be forced. Let go. Let go. Allow the graceful process to unfold.

Epilogue

According to the Torah, the Pishon, the first of the four headwaters issuing out of the river from Eden, "compasseth the whole land of Havilah, where there is gold. And the gold of that land is good; there is the bedolach and the shoham stone." (Genesis 2:10-12). The "Pishon" is the Ganges and the land of "Havilah" is India. Bedolach is believed to be pearls or crystals. The ancient texts of India, such as "The Crest Jewel of Discrimination" and "The Diamond Sutra" liken the purified mind and the wisdom that flows through it to an inner pearl, jewel, or crystal. The Shoham stone is the ancient lingam stone, embodying and reflecting the highest spiritual state and truth of the universal mantra, "Soham", "I am That". One Eastern word designating this highest spiritual state and truth is "Tara".

Consistent with common conceptions, Africa is the mother of civilization and the Middle East is the cradle. Egypt is the womb. Abraham goes down to Egypt to inseminate the womb. He then returns to the area of Palestine, and his first two sons, Isaac and Ishmael, remain there to prepare the land for the nations that are going to develop there. His other six sons are sent to the East/India to further develop the spiritual grounding and wisdom needed to aid the nations that will be descended from their siblings who remain in the area. Jacob follows Abraham's journey to Egypt for a new people to gestate. Moses is sent to aid the Jewish people in birth after a tumultuous nine months of plagues/trials/preparations. The Nile valley is the birth canal. From it emerges this nascent, newly congealed and defined people, the Jewish nation, which is provided direction for its growth and mission through the presentation of the Torah/Tara.

This people is guided to settle in Palestine to mature and develop. They are instructed to conquer/yoke the seven nations residing there, descendants of ancient relatives, representing the seven chakras running up the spine in yoga. In addition to receiving guidance and inspiration from above, they are further instructed to face the East in service and worship. Their brethren, Abraham's six other sons, had previously journeyed there, to develop and emanate rays of wisdom and divine light to be received, concentrated, reformulated and transmitted out to the West.

Through the vehicles of the Tabernacle and Temples, Judaism serves as a prism to convey an East/West message synthesized by Zoroastrianism. A rainbow of religions, cultures and civilizations emerges out of the prism, or are influenced by its emissions. Thus, the Dharma gets transmitted from East to West through this focal point in Palestine.

The most virulent form that the Dharma has taken in the West is the pseudo-religion of liberty-equality-democracy worshiped in the shrines and institutions of the West. Although the New World, led by the United States, has emerged as the premier leader, exemplar and disseminator of this creed, the question remains whether a mature equilibrium, fed by ethical, moral and humanitarian guidelines and considerations, can be established. Or will it continue along certain current lines of juvenile excess and abuse, driven by greed and selfishness, that distort and make a mockery of the values and principles of its founders?

The Dharma still exists in the East and still informs the West, but it is also a two-way street. The West's materialism and scientific advancements inform and influence the East, and likewise, the East's deep spirituality continues to inform and influence the West. Our challenge remains to cultivate and synthesize the best aspects of both worlds while minimizing the worst. What is needed is a continued and concerted effort to create a more mature and harmonious world-wide civilization that celebrates and embraces diversity while recognizing certain principles of underlying unity, basic human dignity, integrity and mutual respect. Globalization needs to do more than merely promote materiality, its attachments and excesses; it needs to provide for the nurturance of spirituality in its many forms.

So be it.

APPENDIX

TORAH STUDY: AN ILLUSTRATION BY A SOMETIMES EXASPERATED STUDENT

To get a sense of what it is like to study Torah and its various translations, interpretations and commentaries, I provide the following example. This is a sample hypothetical sentence and an accompanying sample type of analysis made. Imagine, just about every sentence of the Torah is analyzed along these lines!

(I have found a word used to describe this type of process, used by R. J. Zwi Werblowsky in his chapter on Judaism in *The Concise Encyclopedia of Living Faiths* edited by R. C. Zaehner, and also used by Leo Rosten in an Appendix to *Joys of Yiddish*: "Casuistry", defined by Webster as "subtle but false reasoning, esp. about moral issues; sophistry")

Hypothetical sentence: *"A person drank a glass of water."*

Analysis:

"A": There are questions whether this really was meant as "A", or if properly understood, should be seen as "The". "A person" has a connotation that it is not any particular person, that it could just be any person. However, "The person" would suggest a more specifically identified person, possibly a person previously

identified that is being referred to again. While there is general agreement among the commentators about the significance and meaning of these distinctions between "A" and "The", there is disagreement as to whether "A" as used here really carries the meaning of "The".

"Person": There are differences of opinion among the commentators as to whether this was a male or female or an androgynous personage. Some point to etymological roots favoring an interpretation that it is a male, while others present equally persuasive arguments that it is a female. A third school of thought points to the above disagreement to support its interpretation of an androgynous being, or in the alternative, that the sex is not important. Additionally, there is wide variance of opinion as to whether this was an actual physical being, or meant only in a symbolic sense. There is support for the position that this is a reference to the primordial archetypal human, the Adam Kadmon, while other authorities maintain that there is no such basis for such an interpretation, and that it is a mere reference to a specific physical being, and nothing more. Others maintain that taken within the over-all context, the "person" here is not a reference to a human being at all, whether physical or primordial, but rather is a euphemistic expression for the Divine Personage, and among those with this leaning, there are again differences of opinion whether this is a reference to the Male, Female or Androgynous aspect of the Divine Personage.

"Drank": One issue is whether this was really a past tense event that had occurred and was over and done. Because of the unusual Biblical Hebrew term used, it lends itself to various tense translations, including strictly the past, as translated here, the present ("is drinking"), or even a process transcending or including past, present and future ("drinks"). If it is seen as strictly in the past, it is something that is over and done with. However, if it is seen as presently occurring, there is a sense that it will end at some point. But it can also be seen as an ongoing process that began in the past, is continuing in the present, and will continue for an unknown period of time into the future, perhaps for eternity.

"A": This is the second appearance of this word in this sentence, and carries the same issues on interpretation as discussed above.

"Glass": There is much difference of opinion on exactly the form, size and physical composition of this container. Some commentators say it was made of a material that is no longer known or identifiable, but that is was a clear crystalline-like substance and extremely durable, not unlike our modern tempered glass. Others maintain that it was a much more fragile earthen-ware type of substance, with a reddish-brown hue, similar to red clay. A third school of thought is that it was a metallic substance, either silver or gold, miraculously shaped from a single ingot. Some say it had a delicate shape similar to a champagne flute, while others maintain that it had a sturdy shape, with its base the same diameter as its mouth. An image in between these two extremes is something akin to a goblet, which has been a very common form throughout the ages. The total volume of the container also is subject to many interpretations. Although there is some disagreement, most acknowledge that it probably held three omers, but there is further disagreement as to whether an omer was the volume of 15.2 eggs or 23.6 eggs, and whether they were extra large, large, or medium sized eggs. What most Gentiles don't recognize is that this archetypal image which appears across cultures and time periods, and is portrayed as the Holy Grail in Christian lore, actually had its origins in this word, "glass", as the mystical interpretation for this glass container is that it is the "Cup of Life".

"Of": Believe it or not, there is even significant disagreement here among the Sages. While there is general agreement that the item here is a container, some maintain that it did not contain anything at the time, but rather this "of" is referring to the composition of the container. This school of thought also disagrees with the translation of "drank", maintaining that this term also has the connotation leading to the meaning "took", and that nothing at all was consumed in this event, but rather the empty container was taken in hand to be transported elsewhere. According to this school of thought, the word "water" does not refer to a liquid inside the container, but is a reference to the clear crystalline quality of the substance which comprised the container. Thus the translation would be, "A/the person took a glass/container (made) of a water-like substance." Of course, the more prevalent school of thought is that there was water "in" the container, which in fact was consumed. Hearkening back to the mystical interpretation of the "Cup of Life", we are left with the possibility that the composition of the vessel and its contents, if any, were both comprised of the substance of life, and that perhaps, there is no meaningful distinction to be drawn or that can be drawn between the cup's composition and its contents. Taking this one step further, this can be interpreted as entirely an inner spiritual event, whereby the person is partaking of the inner elixir

of life, and that there was in fact no external physical container at all; the reference to the glass being a reference to the amount of the inner elixir consumed, not to it as a physical entity.

"Water": There are wide variations as to the composition of this substance: sea water, river water, mineral water, spring water, blood and many others. And there are disagreements over whether this was literal, figurative or both. As there is a prohibition against consuming blood, those who support this interpretation urge that it is a symbolic reference to blood as the "staff of life" itself, comparable to the "waters of life", an elixir containing magical, healing, and life-sustaining qualities. On the other end of the spectrum is the school of thought that this was just a plain old glass of water, nothing more, nothing less.

The above illustration raises the question about speculation and authority. What in the commentaries and analysis is just pure speculation, and what has a grounding in some inner guidance and authority? One important distinction is that some of the annotations refer to the Mishnah as the source. Many view the Mishnah as the word of God given to Moses, although initially conveyed verbally and not in writing. So if it is from the Mishnah, it is not speculation, it is authoritative because it is Divine Revelation, as is the Torah. But when commentators start saying, "well, maybe this happened, and maybe that happened", they're speculating, and what is the source for their speculation? Also, how is it that recognized scholars and commentators over the centuries have different interpretations of the same event and speak authoritatively about it? They don't say, "well, maybe this happened". They say, "this is what happened". A lot of these commentators, when they say, "this is what really happened", or "this is what this means", they say it very authoritatively. But you get commentators who disagree with each other. The question is, where is the authority? What is speculation? Why are they speculating? Why can't they say, "well this just isn't clear"? Why do they have to go into all of this speculation?

Perhaps one answer lies in the concept that people at different levels of advancement will interpret things differently, but they may all be true from those different points of view, those different levels. It may be that the person who authoritatively says, "this is what this means, and this is what really happened", at that point in time, that's what they and their students needed to hear. But sometimes there are simultaneous differing points of view. You have warring teachers. In India, there are pandits, gurus and yogis, and a lot of times they disagree. Their followers get into fights over differences in doctrine, authority, spiritual status;

sometimes these differences result in physical altercations. The same thing has always occurred in Judaism and in many religious and spiritual traditions. In Judaism, there was the school of Hillel and the school of Shammai, and the school of this, and the school of that. These guys don't always agree. The existing head of a particular lineage generally follows that lineage, but may also tweak it along the way. The students follow their teachers. They usually keep the disagreements at a level more sophisticated than fist fights. They'll have debates, interchanges, arguments, and they generally conclude that it is okay to agree to disagree, and they leave in relative peace. It may be Hillel and his followers needed to see something one way and interpret it that way, while Shammai and his followers needed to see it the way they saw it. Hillel and Shammai are two famous scholars who lived at the same time, which, interestingly, overlapped with or was in close proximity, to the time of Jesus. Going back to parallels in yoga, there are all different kinds of yoga with different emphases. There is bhakti yoga, jnana yoga, kundalini yoga, hatha yoga, tantra yoga, to name a few. Maybe different predilections, different preferences, are needed for these different paths.

SOURCES

There are various sources upon which Judaism is based. There is the written law, which is the Torah as it appears in the scroll, also known as the Five Books of Moses, the "Pentateuch" in Greek. Then there is the oral tradition. There have been groups that have maintained that there is no validity to the oral tradition; they only believed in the written Torah. The Sadducees and the Karaites were two such groups. In one respect, they could be seen as more fundamentalist in having this limited view, but it some ways it was less restrictive, because there were a lot less rules in the written law; the oral law added many more rules. Most groups have maintained that you can't conceivably understand or follow the written law without the aid and clarification provided by the oral law. I don't know of any current groups who hold the view that there is no validity to the oral law. Certainly, there are groups that question the Divine authenticity and finality of both the written and oral traditions.

Oral traditions often end up getting reduced to writing. The whole idea behind the oral tradition in Judaism was that when the written Torah was originally given to Moses, that was meant to be a summary. It was sort of like a mnemonic device to help remember everything else. As with scriptures in many traditions, it is chanted as a method to memorize it. The additional oral explanation and further explication was also given to Moses at the same time as the written law. Moses came down from the mountain and taught it to the priests and the elders. It was passed on generation to generation among the priests and elders. As in the yoga tradition that incorporates chanting the Vedas, from which mantras are derived, Judaism also had these lineages of sages and rabbis who were passing on this oral law word for word, probably in some kind of singing/chanting fashion, from which many prayers are derived. Supposedly, these people had incredible memories, and could loyally and faithfully remember all of this material, along with the melodies as a mnemonic device that helped them remember it. But it got to a point where there was more dispersion of the people and the scholars, memories weren't as good as in the old days, and there was a concern that the purity was getting lost. So there was a big convocation, around 200 CE/AD, where they got together to write it down before it got lost, and the writing is referred to as the "Mishnah". "Mishnah" comes from a root word meaning "repeat" because it had been repeated from generation to generation among the sages.

The next level is Gemarra, also known as Talmud. The Gemarra originally was a written elaboration of the Mishnah, further commenting and elaborating on the Mishnah. Originally Talmud and Gemarra meant only this written elaboration, but the Mishnah is included in the text of the Gemarra and the Talmud, so now when there is reference to the Talmud, it is generally referring to a work incorporating both the Mishnah and the Gemarra. There were two main versions of the Talmud, the Babylonian and the Jerusalem. The Babylonian is the one that for whatever reason has been much more followed and studied than the Jerusalem. There is overlapping, but also differences, between the two versions. The Talmud is broken up into two main categories: "Halacha", meaning "law" and "the way", and "Aggadah", which are narrative stories illustrating the teachings.

The technicalities in following the commandments is the subject of Halacha. Halacha includes the detailed procedures for conducting ritual slaughter, elaboration of the kosher laws, all the technicalities of how to properly follow the observances and all civil and criminal law. There are Halachic experts who pore over these materials. If there is some technical issue needing to be addressed, one would consult a Halachic expert. There was an issue when an observant Jewish astronaut was going up in the space shuttle. He wanted to maintain his observance of the Sabbath. He would be circling the Earth so many times in a twenty-four hour period. Traditionally, you mark a day from sunset to sunset as one day, and you observe the Sabbath every seventh day. Well, he would be seeing numerous sunsets in a normal twenty-four hour period while orbiting the earth in space! So the question arose whether he should count each sunset to sunset that he observed during space flight as one day in order to determine the seventh day to observe the Sabbath, or should he go by the normal earth time cycles. This was an issue addressed by halachic experts. I think the general consensus was to do it by earth time. There are volumes expounding on halacha.

Aggadah is the tradition of stories and homilies. It would appear that Jesus' use of parables was a form of this homiletic practice. Teachings are illustrated through all kinds of stories. There are frequent citations to the "homiletic" tradition, which is a reference to the Aggadah. Then there is the Passover Haggadah, with an "H" in front of it, which is the most famous. The Passover Haggadah is the story of the Exodus and the prayers that go with it. A lot of this material takes the form of dialogue and conversations between rabbis discussing these fine points. Sometimes they're speaking on behalf of another rabbi, on behalf of a lineage, and sometimes they're speaking for themselves.

Then you have what is called Midrash. Midrash is rabbinic commentaries developed later in time than the earlier sources identified above. So you have commentaries upon commentaries upon commentaries!

There are also common collections in book form. One is called the "Chumash", which contains the Five Books of Moses, selected passages from the Prophets called "Haftorahs", and writings called the five "Megillot". A collection called the "Tanak" corresponds to what Christians call the "Old Testament". It contains the Five Books of Moses, all of the Prophets, and the Holy Writings. The "T" stands for "Torah", the "N" is for the Hebrew word "Nevim", which means "Prophets", and the "K" stands for "Ketuvim", which means, "The Holy Writings". There are a certain number of major prophets, and a certain number of minor prophets, all contained in the book of Prophets. The Holy Writings comprise everything else: The Book of Job, the Book of Esther, the Book of Ruth, Proverbs, Psalms, Song of Solomon, Lamentations, and all of the other contents of the Jewish Scriptural Canon. The Jewish tradition doesn't refer to it as the "Old Testament" because for Jewish people, there is no "New Testament".

"Haftorahs" are selected portions of the Prophets. Along with the practice of reading a Torah portion every week in synagogue, there also developed a tradition to recite a corresponding Haftorah. The Haftorah selection from one of the Prophets usually has some relationship to the Torah portion for that week, although some do not. The origins and practice of reading the Haftorah is one of those things that is lost in the mists of time and mystery. One common conception is that it evolved during periods of persecution, when one method of persecution was to criminalize reading of the Torah, upon severe penalty, including death. The Torah has always been contained in a big scroll, the size of which is designated by official dimensions. It might be possible to make a little Torah, but it wouldn't be an official Torah. It was hard to hide the large Torah scrolls or secret them away quickly if a hostile authority barged in. So when it was difficult to maintain study or reading of the Torah, the Haftorahs were developed as substitutes for summarizing the essence of the teaching of the Torah. The Haftorahs could be contained in a smaller book more easily hidden from persecutors. Although there are a few variations among different groups about some Haftorah portions, there is general agreement on a large majority of them.

Five of the books or scrolls of the Holy Writings are specially designated as the "Megillot", the most popular of which is the Book of Esther, upon which the Purim festival is based.

There are many other commentaries, treatises and writings by scholars and authorities over the years too numerous to mention. Some of the more well-known and influential are the works of Rashi, Onkelos, Maimonides, known as "the Rambam", Nachmanides, known as "the Ramban", Isaac Luria, known as "the Ari", and significant Kabalistic works whose authors are not known or contested, such as the Bahir, the Zohar, and the Sefer Yetzirah.

SUMMARY OF TORAH EVENTS AND PERSONAGES

For the benefit of those who may not have knowledge of or remember much about the content of the Torah, following is a brief summary to assist in providing a point of reference and context for the personages and events discussed in this book.

Genesis is the first book of the Torah, and contains the story of the Creation and all of the "Bible" stories that occur before the time of Moses. The remaining four books of the Torah concern the story of Moses, the Exodus from Egypt, and providing of the law during the forty years of wandering in the desert before entering the Promised Land. All other "Old Testament" stories and materials, such as the stories of the conquest of the Promised Land, Samson, Saul, David, Solomon, the building of the Temple, the Prophets, Psalms, Proverbs, etc., as discussed in the section above on Sources, were assembled at a later time.

The creation of the first man and woman, Adam and Eve, are the culminating acts of creation in Genesis. There are the famous events concerning the temptation by the serpent in the Garden of Eden, resulting in expulsion from the Garden and the slaying of Abel by his brother Cain, the first two sons of Adam and Eve. Seth is a third son born to the original couple, and there is a recitation of events and generations leading from Seth to the time of Noah and the Great Flood, when all of humanity and most living creatures are destroyed except for Noah and his family, and the creatures brought onto the ark (although sources have indicated that more beings than are commonly thought may have survived the Flood).

Although Abraham, considered to be the first Jew, is also commonly thought to be the first monotheist, Shem, Noah's oldest son, actually practiced monotheism and was a High Priest of sorts well before the time of Moses, when the desert Tabernacle was erected and a High Priest and priesthood officially established. The Covenant of the Rainbow which God bestowed upon the survivors of the Great Flood appears to be a heavenly precursor-prism for the Tabernacle and Temples to follow; and the descendants of Noah's three sons, Shem, Ham and Japheth, appear to embody the energies of the middle, right and left pillars, respectively, of a whole earth Tree of Life. Representing balanced middle pillar functioning, Shem was bestowed some type of spiritual/religious mantle of power, and presided over a temple of sorts at the present site of Jerusalem, at that time simply called Salem. Shem passed on this mantle of spiritual power to Abraham, and Abraham propagated the message and teachings of monotheism far and wide. Due to his extensive travels, activities, and acting as a living example of the teachings, Abraham is considered the first Jew and Patriarch of Judaism, and his wife, Sarah, the first Matriarch.

Because Sarah was apparently infertile, when she attained an age beyond child-bearing years she agreed to have Abraham consort with her maidservant, Hagar, who was gifted to them during a trip to Egypt, and they planned to raise the child as their own. Ishmael was thus born to Hagar as Abraham's first son. However, Sarah then miraculously had a son named Isaac. Muslims maintain that Ishmael, who became the progenitor of the Arab race, also assumed the birthright of Abraham. Jews maintain that Isaac assumed this birthright, and thus the early biblical origination of the deep-seated animosity that has existed between Arabs, Muslims and Jews to this day. There is the famous test whereby God demands that Abraham sacrifice Isaac (again, the Muslims say it was Ishmael), only to stop him from carrying out the slaying at the last minute.

In any case, according to the Jewish version, Isaac assumes the mantle from Abraham and becomes the second Patriarch, with his wife Rebecca becoming the second Matriarch. Unlike Abraham before him or Jacob after him, Isaac does not travel out of the area that was later identified as the Promised Land. He remains there and reopens wells that had been dug by Abraham but later closed, and appears to consolidate the energy in the area. Ishmael also remains in the area, fostering a wealth of powerful nations through his offspring and descendants. After Sarah's death, Abraham marries Keturah and has six more sons, who are sent to the East with his gifts, while Isaac and Ishmael remain in the general area of Palestine. Elsewhere in this book is an extensive discussion about these six other sons.

Isaac and Rebecca bear congenital twins, Esau and Jacob, born in that order. Jacob first bargains with Esau to give up his birthright as first born for a cup of stew/lentils, and some time after that follows the famous story of Jacob and Rebecca deceiving the blind Isaac into bestowing the blessing of the Patriarchal lineage intended for Esau upon Jacob, whom Rebecca favored. This double doublecross established a deep animosity in Esau towards Jacob, prompting Jacob to be hustled away by his mother to the land of her brother/his uncle, Laban, to escape Esau's wrath. Right before he began this journey, Jacob had his famous dream/vision at Jerusalem, in which he saw a ladder descending from heaven down to earth, with angels ascending and descending on the ladder, and God spoke with him. Some relate this ladder to a vision of the Tree of Life described in Kabalistic teachings, the same Tree of Life referred to as existing in the Garden of Eden.

Immediately upon arriving in his uncle Laban's land, Jacob romantically falls in love with Laban's daughter/Jacob's cousin, Rachel, but is duped by the devious Laban to first marry his oldest daughter, Leah. Laban exacts from Jacob many years of servitude until he is allowed to marry Rachel. Jacob also takes on two more wives, Zilpah and Bilhah, the maidservents of Leah and Rachel, respectively. While residing in Laban's land, Charan, Jacob fathers twelve of his thirteen children: six sons and one daughter by Leah, one son by Rachel, and two sons by each of the maidservants. Jacob and family eventually slip away into the night after many more years of manipulation and exploitation by Laban. On the way back to the land of his father Isaac, Jacob anticipates a showdown with Esau, and experiences the famous dream/vision in which he wrestles to a draw with an angel of God all night, receiving an injury to his hip, but also the blessing of a new name, "Israel" ("he who wrestles with God and men and prevails"). Esau meets up with Jacob, but instead of war, grants his tearful forgiveness to Jacob, and they go their separate ways in peace.

Next occurs a confounding and controversial story concerning Jacob's daughter, Dinah, but you'll have to look it up yourself for the details!

Jacob's entourage finally makes it to the Promised Land, where Rachel dies giving birth to her second child, which is Jacob's last and twelfth son, Benjamin. They settle down some, but then comes the incident where the next to youngest brother, Joseph, is sold into slavery by his resentful brothers. He and Benjamin had always been favored by Jacob, Joseph had been given a special present of the famous many-colored coat, had tattled on his brothers, and had told them a dream whereby they all bowed to him.

Next is a significant side-story concerning Judah and Tamar, which, like the Dinah episode, you'll just have to look up for yourself.

Joseph ends up as a slave in Egypt, where through many adventures and the gift of being able to interpret dreams, he astonishingly rises to power as second in command to Pharaoh himself. Severe famine strikes the entire area, and due to Joseph's predictions and foresight, Egypt, and especially Pharaoh, is prepared while others are not and become dependent upon Pharaoh. As the first "court Jew", Joseph orchestrates a great concentration of wealth and power in Pharaoh, and Jacob sends his sons on a mission to Egypt for food and supplies. The famous story of the eventual reuniting of Joseph with his family unfolds, and Jacob and his entire entourage settle in Egypt under Joseph's protective wing. Jacob's deathbed blessings of all of his sons and Joseph's two sons breaks the previous one-to-one lineal descent pattern established by Abraham to Isaac to Jacob, with the new lateral designation of these twelve and their descendents as the tribes of Israel. The pure white ray entering the prism thus emerges refracted in a multitude of colors. Jacob is thus considered the last of the three Patriarchs, while Leah and Rachel are ascribed equal status as Matriarchs, although not the maidservant concubines, Zilpah and Bilhah, even though their children are generally ascribed equal tribal status as the children of the two Matriarchs.

The stage is now set for the Exodus story told during the festival of Passover and immortalized in the movie, *The Ten Commandments*. Joseph and the Pharaoh who knew him pass on, a few more generations pass on, and eventually the Hebrews, who lived separately from the Egyptians and had grown in prosperity and numbers, are perceived by the Egyptians as a threat. Privilege turns into slavery, a great cry issues forth, and Moses is designated as the reluctant leader to respond to the call. The particulars of the story of Moses and the Exodus are well known and are not going to be detailed here. Suffice it to say that with the assistance of his brother Aaron and his sister Miriam, after many trials, tribulations and confrontations with Pharaoh, they succeed, against all odds, in leading their people, the descendents of the sons of Jacob/Israel, out of Egypt to freedom and eventual nationhood.

The remainder of the book of Exodus and the two books of Leviticus and Numbers relate events and teachings after the Exodus in the forty years passed in the wilderness (including the reason for the extension of the time to forty years) before crossing the Jordan River to enter the Promised Land. There are battles with hostile peoples in the area. There are many stories of transgression and return, including the well known incidents concerning the Golden Calf and Moses receiving a second set of Ten Commandments tablets after breaking the first, as well as lesser known stories about the ten spies, the rebellion of Korach, the original "talking horse" story, and many others. The 613 commandments are issued (which include civil and criminal law), as are methods for assigning land, establishing judicial systems and purification procedures in cases of ritual impurities. Details are provided for building The Ark of the Covenant to house the Ten Commandment tablets and a portable Tabernacle ("Mishkan") to house the Ark for use in the desert, which will serve as a blueprint for the permanent Temple in Jerusalem to be built later. Likewise, there are details for the vestments of the High Priest, and the first High Priest, Aaron, and his assistant priests (his sons) are invested, but only after a shocking incident where his two eldest sons are killed by Divine Fire for some mysterious transgression of introducing an unauthorized fire. Miriam and Aaron die, and God refutes Moses' entreaties to be allowed to cross the Jordan. Joshua is designated as Moses' successor.

The last book of the Torah, Deuteronomy, is an address by Moses to the people shortly before his death, in which he summarizes all of the events that have transpired and the laws that have been issued, including their meaning and significance, and in which he provides instructions for their future conduct once they cross the Jordan.

THE 613 COMMANDMENTS, THE TEN COMMANDMENTS, AND THE SEVEN NOACHIDE LAWS

There are not only ten commandments in the Torah, there are 613, counting each time that God says to do something or practice some observance (248 positive commandments) or not to do something (365 prohibitions, negative commandments). Over the years, the term for commandment, "mitzvah" (singular form), has also gained the connotation as a "good deed", for the fulfillment of any mitzvah is like a good deed, and several mitzvot particularly are geared towards selflessly serving one's fellow man. Kabbalists have also identified 613 subtle energy channels within the human organism, and it is said that observing a particular mitzvah energizes one of these channels to which it corresponds. Many mitzvot, however, concern matters relating to the existence of the Temple in Jerusalem, so those cannot be observed in modern times after the destruction of the Second Temple and the Diaspora. Some have counted that there are only 339 that can still be observed today, and that it is impossible for any single individual in one lifetime to observe all of those. So there is a conception that observance of the mitzvot is a communal obligation, not solely an individual matter. It is said that it is possible for every individual within a lifetime to observe 270 mitzvot, with 6 that are to be constantly observed on a daily basis: to believe in God, to avow His oneness, to renounce idolatry, to love God, to fear Him, to avoid temptation to sin.

Concerning the Ten Commandments, some sources emphasize that the word "mitzvah", was not used in this context, but rather the word, "dvarim", which more correctly translates as "statements" or "principles". Following are my paraphrased renditions, with some notes. The Ten Commandments are listed twice in the Torah, first in Exodus, and the second time in Deuteronomy, which is Moses' summary of the teachings and events of the Torah immediately prior to his passing. There is one difference between the two versions, as noted.

1. *Constantly remember, and never forget, that there is one God underlying all of existence.*

2. *Do not engage in idolatry.* Do not engage in any belief or practice that even suggests there is more than one God, because if you start down that path, you'll forget the underlying unity of the universe.

3. *Do not take the name of God in vain.*

4. *Remember/Observe the Sabbath.* (It is interesting to note that in the first recital of the Commandments in Exodus, the word "remember" is used, while in the second recital in Deuteronomy, the word, "observe" is used. The comments state the view that "remember" is more a positive commandment of things that are supposed to be done specially on the Sabbath, while "observe" also means "safeguard", and is more a negative commandment of things prohibited from doing on the Sabbath, also in order to set it apart. There is also a view that both meanings are contained in both recitals, although apparently different words are used.

5. *Honor your parents.* (It is interesting that it says "father and mother" and not just "parents").

6. *Do not murder.* (A distinction has been made between murdering and killing another human being, as there are homicides that are not murder, e.g. in self-defense or unintentional, so it is not mere killing/homicide that is prohibited, but only murder/unjustified criminal killing).

7. *Do not commit adultery.* (The comments note that by definition, this meant sexual relations between a married woman and someone other than her

husband, and it would be only the woman who would be guilty of adultery, and not her partner).

8. *Do not steal.* (To my surprise, the notes maintain that this only relates to one form of theft subject to capital punishment: a kidnapper who forces his victim to work for him and then sells him into slavery. Supposedly other forms of theft are prohibited by others of the 613 mitzvahs, but not this one).

9. *Do not bear false witness.* (The notes say this includes gossip and slander).

10. *Do not covet/envy.* (It is interesting that this commandment goes on in specific detail not present in the others: "do not covet your fellow's house, wife, manservant, maidservant, ox, donkey, nor anything that belongs to him." Why so specific about the ox and donkey? The notes are silent about this, but do point out another peculiarity: "coveting" doesn't seem to carry the gravity of the offenses of many of the other commandments. It lies in a different realm of subtlety, but is nonetheless extremely important as a matter of faith: if God has determined that someone else has something, it is none of our business to even think twice that we should have it instead.)

Concerning the Seven Noachide Laws, or "The Seven Instructions of Noah", unlike the Ten Commandments, there is no place in the Torah where these are explicitly enumerated. Talmudic sources extrapolated from the Torah text that the numerous commandments identified above were intended for observance only by the Jewish people in order to fulfill their specific mission, but among these were included seven universal laws intended for guidance and observance by all of mankind to assure a righteous and harmonious earthly life. They are associated with Noah, as they are considered to have been included in the terms of the covenant of the rainbow that God made with Noah after the Great Flood. They apply to all of mankind, because we are all descended from Noah. Some sources have argued that God's direction to conquer the seven Canaanite nations residing in the Promised Land at the time of the Exodus did not mean to eradicate or expel all of them, but only those who did not covenant to obey these seven laws.

1. *Acknowledge that there is only one God who is infinite and Supreme above all things.* (This incorporates not engaging in idolatry).

2. *Respect the Creator.* (This incorporates not taking the name of God in vain).

3. *Do not murder.*

4. *Respect the institution of marriage.* (This incorporates not committing adultery).

5. *Do not steal.* (This incorporates the broader definition of a prohibition against theft of all kinds).

6. *Respect God's creatures.* (This relates to the permission to eat meat provided after the Great Flood. It is more specifically worded as a prohibition against removing and eating a limb from a live animal, but it has been construed to incorporate procedures for humane slaughtering, and generally treating animals humanely).

7. *Maintain justice.* (This includes establishing temporal rules of law and procedure. It incorporates not bearing false witness, not coveting, and some say it also incorporates honoring one's parents).

As can be seen, many of the Ten Commandments are incorporated in the Noachide Laws and vice-versa. Observing the Sabbath is one commandment not included, and some say that honoring one's parents is not included, while others say it is included in maintaining justice. The only Noachide Law not included in the Ten Commandments concerns respecting animals, but that principle is covered in detail by the many other mitzvot and kosher laws concerning the slaughter of animals for either sacrifice, consumption, or both.

KOSHER LAWS

There is a general outline given in the Torah enumerating specific things that can and cannot be eaten. There are also additional rules, regulations and other rituals that have been developed for the preparation, cooking and consumption of certain foods that are allowed to be eaten. For example, you can eat beef, but you can only eat beef if it is slaughtered, blessed, prepared and cooked in a certain way. That is all part of the koshering process. The Jewish view is that before Noah, everyone was vegetarian, and after Noah, God allowed people to eat meat under the prescribed conditions. Vegetarians are close to automatically keeping kosher, because, except for a few technical issues, there don't appear to be koshering rules concerning non-meat foods, perhaps because they were always allowed to be consumed before the koshering laws came into existence.

In traditional Jewish thought, blood is life. You don't want to compromise human life in any way. That's why Orthodox Jews will not take a blade in any way to their skin. They will not cut, tattoo, or pierce, because you don't want to compromise blood/life-force/prana in any way whatsoever. Concerning donating blood, that would be one of those interesting questions for the halachic authorities. There is one law that overrules just about every other law, and that is if a law needs to be broken in order to save a life, that consideration overrules everything else. I don't know if Orthodox Jews would give blood or not. Certainly, non-Orthodox Jews give blood. But I would think that even the Orthodox would say that if this is helping someone live, then it's okay to do it, but perhaps not in just a practice of donating blood in a blood drive, because the life-saving there is too remote; the threat of losing a life is not imminent. Certainly, I would think if an Orthodox Jew was confronted with a situation that if he or she did not give blood, then another person right there and then would most likely die, then I think they would give the blood. There are two exceptions to the rule that breaking any other law is okay if it means saving a life: you can't save a life if it means taking another life, and you can't commit incest even if somehow doing so would save another life. But any of the other commandments can be broken if breaking it would help save a life, because saving a life is a higher commandment than almost anything.

The reasoning behind the practice of not compromising human blood, if at all possible, carries over to the koshering laws concerning the proper preparation for the consumption of meat. There are rules and regulations on how to slaughter and cook meat, guided by the notion that you aren't supposed to consume blood because doing so would be to ingest lower animalistic life force, nature and instincts. These dictates ran contrary to common ancient practices of consuming blood of humans and animals for the very reason shunned by the kosher laws: those practitioners saw value in invigorating one's own life force by ingesting and sacrificing the life force of others. One significant aspect to the contrary Jewish practice is to control, redirect, sublimate, transform, transmute the lower animal nature within us, not to enliven or glorify it. That is the basis for the animal sacrifices at the Temple; they were symbolic of sacrificing the inner animal nature. One can imagine what the Temple was like during these sacrifices; it was like a slaughterhouse. There was a place where the blood was poured for its return to the earth, except for instances when some of the blood was sprinkled upon those assembled, for reasons I have not yet discovered. In other instances, the carcass and all of its blood was to be fully incinerated by flame, leaving nothing but ashes. But all of the blood had to go, one way or another.

The kosher laws concerning the consumption of meat include specifying the methods for the slaughter, preparation and cooking of the meat. The use of salt in the process is meant to draw out as much blood as possible. But what we refer to as the "juice" in meat is really considered the remnants of the blood by many

Orthodox, although Chabad has a differing view. The solution for those not subscribing to the Chabad view is that meat is always supposed to be cooked well done, to cook off the juice. An Orthodox Jew cannot enjoy a nice juicy steak. It may not taste as good or be as tender, but that is the idea.

One alternative to meat being cooked until it is well-done, rendering it tough, is the common traditional Jewish practices of making stews and of pickling, smoking, turning meat into cold cuts and things like that. It is interesting that in the Agni Yoga texts, whereby the Mahatmas were communicating through the Roerichs, vegetarianism is strongly encouraged. There are sections in those texts where it directs that if you are going to eat meat, eat dried, smoked or pickled meat. Get the blood out of there, minimize consumption of animal life force contained in the blood. So from another tradition that appears quite removed from Judaism, we find a parallel consistent with this Jewish practice to remove and not consume the blood. Another fundamental kosher law is that you're not supposed to eat milk in the same meal with meat. That comes from one phrase in the Torah where it says, "don't cook the kid in its mother's milk". That one phrase has promulgated extensive rules to assure that dairy and meat are not mixed. Any type of milk product or food containing milk should not be consumed in the same meal with meat. There are supposed to be so many hours between consuming milk and meat. This also generated a requirement to maintain separate sets of dishes for dairy and meat foods, to assure that no particles, no remnants of milk and meat are ever mixed.

Kosher laws totally prohibit consumption of certain kinds of animal flesh. Prohibited are pork and shellfish, allowed are fish with gills and scales. If it doesn't have gills and scales, which means most seafood and shellfish as opposed to fish – shrimp, lobster, crab, scallops, clams, oysters – it is prohibited. The general rule concerning four-legged animals is the flesh of animals that chew their cud *and* have split hooves is allowed. Horsemeat is prohibited because horses don't have split hooves. Pigs have split hooves, but they don't chew their cud, so pork is prohibited. Pork has always been singled out, maybe because it has been pointed out that pigs and hogs are a little more devious in their structure. It is easy to detect the many unkosher animals that do not have split hooves. Apparently, pigs and hogs are the only animals that have split hooves but do not chew their cud, so they're not kosher. It takes a little more digging to ascertain that they don't chew their cud. Concerning birds, a possible criterion has been noted that scavengers and birds of prey are generally prohibited, as with seafood, of which many types are likewise scavengers. The Torah even specifies in some detail insects that can and cannot be eaten. The authorities cannot identify all of the animals or insects discussed because of the archaic names used.

While there have been attempts to provide rational bases for the kosher laws, on a spiritual level, one Orthodox explanation is that there may be no humanly rational basis, despite the commentators' efforts to provide one. There is one category of law in Torah by which some authorities concede that nobody will ever figure out a rational basis. This category of law is commonly translated as a "decree". God said do it or don't do it, and don't even ask any questions, you'll never figure it out. It's on a spiritual level. I have even come across Orthodox sources that concede that on a physical level, although there have been health issues concerning pork carrying more potential for disease than beef, if pork is properly prepared, it is no more harmful than beef. Their contention is that it is only significant on a more subtle spiritual level. Why? We don't have any idea. God said don't do it, and we're not going to do it, and leave it at that. Another example of a decree that appears to have no humanly rational basis is "the law of the red cow". This law has achieved some prominence in recent years because it has become associated with messianic movements. Most commentators don't try to explain the practices concerning the red cow, because they are so bizarre. The authorities contend that most laws have some rational explanation, but for this genre called "decrees", don't even ask. That's the basic explanation. God commanded it, and that's good enough for us.

Part of Orthodoxy is a tendency to become obsessed with all of these rules and regulations. There is almost a neurotic obsession with the rules, and if you break a rule, what you have to do to atone for it. There are halachic experts who pore over the main rules that are laid out in the Torah and all of the analysis, interpretation and commentary that have been added over the centuries by the rabbis and scholars.

MOVEMENTS/BRANCHES OF JUDAISM

Judaism has developed what are generally referred to as "movements" or "branches". The nomenclature is a sensitive issue; there is an aversion to use of the word "denominations". The Orthodox are quick to point out that before the early 1800's, they were the only game in town. However, even among the Orthodox, there have always been many different subdivisions, although not denominated as "movements" or "branches". One historical difference that has faded away over the centuries is illustrated by the differences between the Pharisees and the Sadducees in Jesus' time. The Sadducees believed only in the sanctity of the written Torah text; they did not believe in the Mishnah, the oral law that existed but had not yet been reduced to writing. They maintained that all that counted was the written text of the actual Torah, and nothing else. The Pharisees believed in the oral commentary. On its face, it would appear that the Sadducees were more strict and fundamentalist in their view that only that which is written is definitive. But in some respects, the opposite in practice was true. The oral commentaries set forth with specificity many observances, laws and restrictions that were only very generally alluded to in the written text. So the Pharisees in practice, with all of the additional oral strictures, were more strict and Orthodox in their observances. The Sadducees were actually a lot looser, because they didn't subscribe to all of the constrictions that developed through the oral tradition. There were other sects, such as the Karaites, that also did not believe in the oral tradition. So even within Orthodoxy going way back in time, there have been all kinds of distinctions and arguments about what should be observed, what is true, what isn't true, etc.

Hasidism, a movement now viewed as a type of Orthodoxy, started in the 1700's. The originator was Israel ben Eleazar, who became known as "The Bal Shem Tov", "The Master of the Good Name". He was like a Jewish Zen Master. During the time that he lived in Russia, traditional Judaism had become very rigid. There were lineages of rabbis along familial lines that had control over the communities. There was an emphasis on study, scholarship, and developing detailed expertise in the intricacies of law and observance, resulting in an elitist class. They had lost touch with the common people, who had no source for spiritual and religious inspiration. So the Hasidic movement, founded by the Bal Shem Tov, came along to address needs that weren't being met. It was in some ways like a radical reformation movement, claiming, "You don't need all of this rabbinic authority. You don't need to study all of these books. It doesn't have to be grim. It can be joyful. You can do it yourself." There were personages like the Bal Shem Tov and his successors called "Rebbes" as opposed to "rabbis". They were like these Zen Masters within Judaism; they were inspiring, charismatic leaders. Extraordinary, magical, mystical events and powers were associated with them, along with down-to-earth practical wisdom. They were regarded in a way that is remarkably similar to the ways disciples in the yoga tradition regard their gurus. These "tzadiks", as they were called, these enlightened, righteous, highly elevated beings, became the leaders of movements separate from the normal Orthodox movement of the time. You were supposed to pay penance to the Orthodox rabbis and go to their synagogues. Then the Hasidim came along and said, you don't need to go to their synagogues, we'll do our own services.

The Hasidic movement became very popular in Eastern Europe in areas such as Germany, Russia and Poland. The traditional Orthodox authorities came close to excommunicating these people. In fact, one major Orthodox authority at the time, known as the Vilna Goan, actually did excommunicate the Hasidim. He and other Orthodox authorities claimed the Hasidim weren't Jewish, that the Jewish community should have nothing to do with them, as they had nothing to do with Judaism. They were radical reformers and an obvious threat to the status quo. However, Hasidism persisted and was so appealing that it survived all of the early ostracism. The early split between Hasidism and non-Hasidic Orthodox today is minimalized. There are different movements even within Hasidism, but despite their differences, the various Hasidic sects are all now about as Orthodox as anybody. Although they started out as a revolution, an extreme and radical reformation against the Orthodoxy that existed at the time, today, many would consider them the epitome of ultra-Orthodoxy.

However, there are still distinctions between the traditional Orthodox and the Hasids. The Hasidim are more spiritually and mystically oriented. I have discovered many fascinating insights and information from their sources and commentaries that I have not found from traditional sources and commentaries. There are doctrinal differences between Hasidism and traditional Orthodox, mostly stemming from the mysticism that is a key component in Hasidism, which has been largely de-emphasized and ignored by the traditional Orthodox. For example, Hasidism subscribes to a conception of reincarnation whereas traditional Orthodox does not. It's been interesting for me to explore Hasidic thought, because of the many parallels I see with yoga mysticism.

With the possible exceptions noted above, until the early 1800's, the differences that existed within Judaism would generally be considered variants within Orthodoxy. It wasn't until the early 1800's that more distinct movements started to develop, with the first one being the "Reform" movement that started in Germany. They probably received an impetus from the Protestant Reformation movement. The original Reform movement was extremely radical – in many respects, much more radical than what Jesus taught in relation to the prevalent Jewish thought of his time. The Reform rejected a fundamental Orthodox creed that the Torah is Divine Revelation, the actual word of God. Their idea, incorporated in academic circles as the "Redaction Theory", is that the Torah and related scriptures are significant, but nevertheless, man-made texts pieced together over a period of time, like a cut-and-paste job. These texts, even though inspired, were man-made, had multiple authors, existed here, there and everywhere, were tampered with, revised and edited over a lengthy period of time, eventually resulting in what we have today. Different authors had different agendas. It's obvious that the texts are very male-oriented. It is similar to the kind of critical analyses of the New Testament that exists in certain circles. Basically, the Reform said, "We have our identity as Jewish people, but we reject much of the traditional Orthodox theology. We still want to do some of the practices, conduct some services, observe some holidays; we still want to retain our identity as Jews, but we're throwing out a lot of the traditional observances and beliefs." It was and remains very radical compared to Orthodox, although there have been over time some significant shifts away from the extreme original radical beliefs and practices and movement back towards more conservatism. The Orthodox still sort of hold their breath about it. There isn't a whole lot of excommunication in Judaism. There have been a few instances, one being the actions of the Vilna Goan concerning the Hasidim described above, and another famous one being the Orthodox excommunication of the philosopher Baruch Spinoza. But to the Orthodox, even though not excommunicated, the Reform are virtual heretics.

It is clear from studying a history of the Reform movement, that in addition to wanting to express and establish a faith with genuine doctrinal differences from the Orthodox, it was also an attempt at a remedial response to centuries of relentless persecution suffered by the Jewish people. The Reform movement was an attempt to be better accepted by the dominant Christian society from where it originated. The message to European Christian society was clear: "Look. We're going to be and appear and conduct ourselves as Christian as we possibly can, but we still want to maintain our Jewish identity." What the Reform do, how they do it, what their beliefs are, what their practices are, is all geared towards trying to blend with the modern industrial societies of Europe and America. Before the Reform movement, the main solutions to persecution were either to hold fast and just bear with it or assimilate. Reform came up with a new alternative solution of maintaining some Jewish identity while at the same time trying to reduce the differences with their Christian neighbors. The Reform method and message was, "We're really not all that different. We're eliminating skullcaps, long beards and sideburns. Look, we eat pork and shellfish! Come to our services. They almost look like church services. Yes, we throw around a little bit of Hebrew, but it is mostly in English. And yes, we don't talk about Jesus because we choose to focus on the Old Testament." If you attend a Reform temple service, it looks and feels a lot more like a church service than what you will encounter at an Orthodox service. The Reform for a while even eliminated Bar and Bat Mitzvahs in favor of a more Christian-like "Confirmation" for its puberty-related rite of passage, including advancing the age for its celebration. But the emotional connection with Bar and Bat Mitzvahs was so strong that they have made a comeback, in addition to, or instead of, the alternative Confirmation process. So Reform in large part was an expression of a need to want to be part of the larger society and not be separate, but still retain some separate identity ethnically and religiously.

Next came the Conservative movement, which tried to reconcile and synthesize the two extremes of Orthodox and Reform in both form and substance, and strike a middle ground balance between the two. Maybe part of the Torah is authentic Divine Revelation, and maybe part of it has been dabbled with a little bit by human intervention. It tried to incorporate some of the Orthodox and some of the Reform and create something in the middle.

There are other movements, including Modern Orthodox, Neo-Orthodox, Traditional and Reconstructionism. There's something called the "Jewish Renewal" and related "Havurah" movements, which lean towards the Reform side, but preserve more of the traditional.

Bigger differences between the movements are found in the realm of ritual and observances concerned primarily with an individual's relationship with God and their own spiritual well-being. The Orthodox have observances that they derive from the Torah in following all of the commandments, physically and literally. Many of those have been subject to rejection or modification by the various reform movements. You go to a Reform temple, and you'll see an abbreviated form of the Orthodox service. They may render traditional prayers more egalitarian by making more references to the Matriarchs. They simplify it and use a lot more English and different melodies. Orthodox worship remains totally or predominantly in Hebrew. Conservatives are in between. During various phases, elements of the non-Orthodox movements have ranged from quite radical to more conservative; traditional sources and scriptures have at differing times been almost fully rejected, minimized, or acknowledged. Among most movements, in more recent times there has been a swing back to drawing from the traditional sources, but different branches continue to draw on them from varying perspectives. There is probably less emphasis in the non-Orthodox movements on messianism.

There are lesser differences between the movements in the realm of practical morality and ethics concerned with the individual's relations to their community and fellow human beings. In these respects, the distinctions between the different movements are much more blurred. The ethical and moral dictates that derive from the Torah, such as honoring your fellow man, loving your neighbor, practicing charity, all of those kind of basic moral and ethical precepts are taught and followed regardless of the movement.

Even to this day, people in Orthodoxy do not recognize anybody outside of Orthodoxy as being legitimate practicing Jews. According to Orthodoxy, if you're born Jewish, you're Jewish. But they wouldn't recognize a Bar Mitzvah by a Reform or a Conservative as a legitimate Bar Mitzvah. Another area where it comes into play is that Reform or Conservative converts are not recognized as being Jewish by the Orthodox. This is particularly significant concerning the State of Israel's "Law of Return", which provides that any Jew who so desires is granted Israeli citizenship by virtue of being Jewish. As Orthodoxy is the only recognized Jewish movement in Israel, non-Orthodox converts are not granted Israeli citizenship under the Law of Return.

Another important doctrinal distinction among the movements involves the notion of "The Chosen People". This Orthodox doctrine was part of the reason for all the persecution throughout the ages. Reform and Reconstructionism repudiate or minimize it, while Orthodoxy embraces it. Orthodoxy maintains that what is contained in the Torah scroll is infallible Divine Revelation, while others view it as just another book, or perhaps a special book, but not of infallible Divine origin.

Another interesting issue concerns the belief in a Jewish State, Israel, also referred to as "Zion". A "Zionist" is someone who believes in a Jewish State. There have been all kinds of splits on this matter. There were people in Orthodoxy who did not support creating a Jewish State by mortal means, as it was actually accomplished. They believed that a Jewish State should only be created when the Messiah appears. That is now a minority view, but it was and still is a view. There were people who were totally non-observant who were nevertheless, from an ethnic point of view, avid Zionists. Many of the people who were instrumental in bringing into existence the current State of Israel were cut of this cloth. They had hardly any religious persuasion. They were largely East European socialists and communists. Most Orthodox now support the State of Israel, although there are Orthodox extremists who desecrate the graves of Theodore Herzl and David Ben Gurian, two key figures involved in the creation of the State of Israel.

It is curious that the only Jewish movement recognized in Israel is Orthodoxy, and they seem to have a clamp on it, along with political clout. It is interesting, as noted above, that many Orthodox originally did not like the idea of humans without a Messiah leading the way to the creation of the State of Israel. Even early in the Zionist movement, there was one secular faction that promoted creating a Jewish State in a location other than the land of Palestine. They knew from the beginning that there were going to be problems in the physical location of Palestine. This movement wanted to create a State of Israel in some uninhabited grasslands in Africa, in Uganda, when it was still controlled by the British. That idea fell by the wayside in favor of proponents who insisted that it had to be located in the politically-charged hotbed of Palestine, for all of the religious, mythic reasons designating that area as the Promised Land, the Land of Milk and Honey. As earlier addressed in this book, it seems to be the locus of an apex of significant energy, at a major crossroads of the world. Once the modern State of Israel became an actuality, many of those who initially opposed it for varying reasons, along with most Jewish people of any persuasion, now generally support its continued existence in its current location. There remain, however, deep tensions and emotional differences among the various political and religious factions within Israel as to boundaries and possible co-existence with a Palestinian state.

Concerning egalitarian issues among the various branches of Judaism, the Orthodox have their own explanations as to why it appears to be very patriarchal and male-oriented, explanations that many women and men have difficulty accepting. The basic Orthodox point of view is that women are so much more closely attuned with Divinity than men, that they don't need to go to the synagogue and do all of the things that only men are allowed or authorized to do. It is not so much that the men have these special entitlements, it is more that the men have these additional obligations and burdens not imposed upon the women. I don't know if originally women were even allowed to go to synagogue at all. If they go now, they are separated from the men and they can't go onto the pulpit. The real Orthodox still don't recognize Bat Mitzvahs for women. But the Orthodox explanation is that women don't need that because women are so much more spiritually pure than men. All of those extra obligations are designed to turn the men away from their lower animal instincts and keep them focused on the straight and narrow. By virtue of being capable of bearing life, and for other reasons, women, by their very nature, are more closely aligned with Divinity.

The Reform response to the Orthodox point of view concerning the role of women is "balderdash!". Women have a right to a piece of the liturgical action, to go onto the pulpit, to become rabbis, to be Bat Mitzvah. Prayers referencing any of the patriarchs should reference the corresponding matriarch at the same time. Let's not forget or slight Woman. Let's not forget the role of the female energy in all of this. There are currently significant movements within some branches of Judaism to institute an equal place for women and the feminine principle. The "Shekinah" – which is very similar to the yogic Kundalini Shakti conception of a magnified, concentrated female power – is what communicated from the Ark. Shekinah is considered the female aspect of Divinity, that which is capable of dwelling among us, often just referred to as *the* Divine Presence, while neglecting to emphasize its female nature. So even in traditional Orthodoxy, as in yoga, although it is not emphasized, there is an underlying acknowledgement that at the primordial levels of creating, sustaining, and dissolving, nothing becomes manifest, nothing is sustained, and no dynamic progress is possible without the Female. The Mother Divine is from whom everyone and everything manifests, and nothing can happen without the function of the Mother Divine. The Shekinah is the real energy that is emanating and telling the world what to do and how to do it. When the High Priest went into the Holy of Holies to seek inspiration and guidance, he was communing with the Shekinah, the Matriarchal, the Feminine Principle.

All Jewish movements generally observe the same major holidays. Some of the holidays were explicitly delineated in the Torah. Others have been added since then. There are a few major holidays and many more lesser holidays. In Judaism, if you observed all of the holidays, almost every day would be some holiday! The major holidays are observed from a religious, ethnic or cultural point of view, but observing them is still considered of value. Anyone who considers themselves a practicing or observant Jew in some way or another is going to observe the basic major holidays. The more Orthodox one is, the greater the quantity of the lesser holidays that will be observed, and the more stringent will be the observances.

I saw on an Orthodox web site the results of a survey that is periodically conducted of people who consider themselves Jewish and practicing Jews in some form or another. The survey asks the respondents to identify their movement affiliations, or how they view themselves based upon the loose definitions of the various movements. The general breakdown is about thirty percent conceive of themselves as Orthodox and the other seventy percent is split between Reform and Conservative. It seems to me that Orthodox literature and teachings are generally more prevalent and accessible in the public domain. Maybe the Orthodox just work at it harder. It seems like it is more difficult to find books, teachings and websites authored by Reformists. The thinking, the teaching, the propagating seems to be dominated by Orthodox proponents. Various Orthodox movements seem more aggressive than their counter-parts in other movements in "missionary" work of attempting to "convert" non-observant Jews, although it remains an Orthodox practice to discourage conversion by non-Jews. Yet the majority of people who consider themselves Jewish don't consider themselves Orthodox; they consider themselves somewhere in that split between Conservative and Reform. I think it is largely because they are not accepting of all of the Orthodox notions and observances. They think you can still be a good practicing Jew without having to follow all of the mitzvot and halacha to the literal extremes espoused by the Orthodox.

PERSECUTION

I have previously touched upon the theme of persecution, and it is not something I dwell on. However, I think that no book about Judaism would be complete without a little more thorough review of Jewish persecution, as it is a pervasive element in most Jews' psyches. It is true that Christians historically have persecuted all kinds of groups, including subdivisions of Christianity. But Jews still hold a significant place in the Christian psyche, because Jews have been singled out as killing Jesus. In addition, just about *everybody* has persecuted Jews. I have never been one that's identified with all of that too much. It has been part of the culture that I grew up with, this heritage of persecution and victimization. My attitude has usually been, "Let it go already. Let's just get on with life". But as part of my studies, I read the acclaimed history by Paul Johnson, a modern British historian, called *The History of the Jews*. He's Christian, but he became captivated with Judaism. He said that he didn't realize until he got into his research how much Christianity owed to Judaism and how much of a foundation still exists. He's an intellectual, an academic historian, and he certainly isn't into the mystical aspects, going so far as to denigrate them. He respects the religious aspects, but he snubs Kabala.

In one chapter, Johnson relates centuries of persecution in some detail. If it's not by the Christians, it's by the Moors. If it's not in France, it's in Spain. If it's not in Spain, it's in Italy. It goes on and on. He's presenting the history in an objective fashion, not in an emotionally sympathetic manner. He's just factually presenting how it was. It was difficult reading through it all. It has given me more of an understanding as to how long it went on and the many insidious forms it took. There were occasional periods of relief. Sometimes there would be a more enlightened and liberal overlord. There would be a broad-minded Moorish overlord, and there would be a wonderful symbiotic relationship established; a Jewish community would flourish under a Moorish ruler. A substantial Jewish community and kabalistic tradition developed in Spain under Moorish rule, with intriguing cultural and spiritual interchanges. But then a fundamentalist, Taliban-like new ruler would come along and all of a sudden, the honeymoon was over. The same thing happened with Christianity. There would be enlightened Christian rulers who appreciated how the Jews were fitting in and contributing to their society. They overlooked discriminatory regulations against the Jews. But then someone new would come into power, and all of a sudden, the persecutions would start all over again.

The sense I obtained from reading this history was that even during the benevolent times, there was understandably a certain angst, a looking over the shoulder, a wondering of "how long is this going to last?" There were always reasons or excuses for resentment or envy to develop. It was a repeating vicious cycle. For example, the Torah says that there is a prohibition against money-lending, meaning you can't charge interest on loans. The idea was that if someone was in such need that they would stoop to the humiliating level of seeking to borrow money, it wasn't proper to inflict pain on them, to kick them when they were down, by charging interest. Make a loan, get it back when you can, and move on. To exact a benefit from someone else's dire straits was considered improper, immoral. But the prohibition only applied to fellow Jews; it was okay to charge interest to a non-Jew. The Christian tradition incorporated the moral teaching against charging interest to your fellow man. For a long time in the Christian world, it was improper, immoral, sinful, the work of the Devil, to charge interest to anybody. However, the pragmatic Christian leaders saw that nevertheless, there was a commercial benefit to be derived from money-lending.

In modern times, high finance is not a response to an individual's need, but rather a practice that promotes economic corporate growth. Even in the Middle Ages, the commercial usefulness of loans with interest was beginning to be recognized. The Christian observance of the dictate against charging interest on loans was causing a detrimental effect on commerce; they wouldn't loan money to each other at interest in circumstances that would otherwise stimulate and benefit commerce, and they would only make interest-free loans in cases of genuine charitable need. Well, the Christian rulers decided to let the Jews do it, because their Torah permitted charging interest to non-Jews. They struck a deal with the Jewish community: we're going to let you charge interest to non-Jews because it's going to help our commerce, but we're going to take some of your profits through taxes! The Jews were always taxed more than anyone else. They were allowed to money-lend, the rulers got half of the profits, and it stimulated commerce. But at some point, someone fundamentalist would come along and determine it was all highly improper, the Jews were taking unfair advantage, and the axe would fall again. Thus developed the reputation of Jews being greedy, despicable money-lenders.

Another cause for possible resentment of Jews is something I have sensed relating to mysticism and its abuses, although Johnson doesn't discuss it much. Jews developed a very elaborate and detailed system of mysticism. Along with it came the "practical" or applied side of occult arts and superstitious practices. My sense is that a lot of the occultism and black magic practiced in Medieval Europe and elsewhere had its roots in Jewish and Christian Kabala. For people who were not privy to these matters steeped in mystery and secrecy, it was threatening and frightening. Whether it was benevolent or not benevolent did not matter. Benevolent practices tend to get abused. One reason for keeping mystical practices secret is to prevent abuse. But going back a few hundred years, things started opening up, and Christians got exposed to Kabala, including development of mystical powers, conjuring, and creating golems (humanoid creatures). The Frankenstein story actually has its roots in Kabala. Aryeh Kaplan in his book on the Sefer Yetzirah refers to incantations used to create golems. I believe this resulted in a fear of occultism and its abuses, which formed part of the basis for the persecutions.

Paul Johnson noted in his history that Christianity and Islam appear to be the most imperialistic religions. Most other religions acknowledge that there are other valid religions. It is Christianity and Islam particularly that maintain that theirs is the only one true religion. Everyone else has to convert or else! Convert or we'll kill you. Convert or die. Your choice. But there was a catch for those who did convert: they were persecuted anyway because the sincerity of their conversion was questioned. It was another no-win situation. The issues arising from perceived or real insincere conversions resulted in other solutions: Inquisitions and expulsions, the most infamous ones being in Spain and Portugal during the time of Christopher Columbus.

TORAH STUDY: RANDOM THOUGHTS ON VARIOUS THEMES AND ISSUES

Male and Female

Now, what about the male and female in traditional and mystic Judaism? It seems in studying the traditional sources that there was certainly a male dominant hand involved in structuring most of these materials. There are all kinds of explanations for the traditional roles of male and female. The traditional orthodox observance, which I never knew was so extreme, is a human female and a human male are never supposed to touch each other physically unless they are married, with the exception of parents, their children, and siblings. Other than that, when a couple courts, there is no touching. Women are now being allowed greater access to certain programs and they can participate on an equal basis as men in the programs. Women now are allowed to and even being encouraged to study. From that point of view, there appears to be more openness to women. The Orthodox still don't allow women on the bimah, the pulpit, in a synagogue. Real Orthodox don't perform Bat Mitzvahs for girls, only Bar Mitzvahs for boys. There was an innovation of having Bat Mitzvahs for girls in less orthodox practices and more Orthodox have been recognizing Bat Mitzvahs. So there may be some inroads, but there are still many strict traditional observances.

Although there certainly appears to be a dominant male orientation throughout the ages in Judaism, there has always been an undercurrent about the importance and significance of the female. The Kabalistic conception is that nothing can exist without the female because the female *is* existence. Everything in existence is female because everything in existence is *form* of some sort or other; even if it is strictly on an energy level, energy is still form. And all form is female. On the other hand, pure unfettered consciousness or force is the province of the male, which cannot be expressed in any way without the form of the female. The Shekinah communicating from between the two Cherubim on the Ark is female because it is expression of some sort. Obviously there is a definite importance to the female because nothing exists without the female. This is very similar to the formulations of Tantric Yoga of the male aspect exemplified by Shiva, and the female aspect exemplified by Shakti.

Orthodox Jews say they honor the female and that all of the outsider criticisms are unfounded, that their critics just don't understand the proper role of the female in life. The kitchen is holier than the pulpit, but the kitchen is where the female is supposed to be. The traditional Jewish view is that women are much more in touch with the Divine by their nature and don't need to study and go to prayer the way that men do. Men need to study because men are more easily led astray and off the path. Women are much more connected with the Divine just by virtue of being women, by virtue of having the ability to give birth, so they don't need to go and pray three times a day. So they can stay in the kitchen and cook and serve their husbands and families. They may appear to be treated as second class citizens, but that is a misperception, a misunderstanding. That is the Orthodox point of view.

There are issues concerning feminine impurity, especially at the time of the menses. There is a taboo of not going near a woman during her period. There is something called a "mikvah" that has become associated mostly with use by women where they are basically segregated until they are purified and free of their menses. I don't know if it is used for many other purposes these days, but traditionally, the mikvah was holy water in which Jews would immerse themselves for purposes of cleansing all kinds of spiritual impurities. Some types of impurity was caused by straying, by sinning. Other types were not due to sinning; they were caused by circumstances that were unavoidable in daily material living. For example, in addition to menstruation, touching a corpse caused impurity, but it was a necessity; someone had to deal with the dead. So men used mikvahs too. There was constantly a need to cleanse, to purify oneself through this process. You got schmutz on yourself, you became impure, so you needed to cleanse. I don't know if there is still much use by men, or if that ended after the destruction of the Second Temple or some other time. The Christian practice of baptism likely has its origins in the Jewish use of the mikvah. Baptism, as it was originally used by John the Baptist, was for cleansing, for purification, for renewing. A river could qualify as a mikvah, and it may have been common during those times to use a river as a mikvah. It is similar to Hindu practices of performing ablutions in a river or in a "tank", a pool of incorporated into most temple complexes.

There are many current movements, led, most appropriately, by Jewish women and female rabbis, to rediscover the role and importance of women and the female within Judaism. Traditionally, there are rarely references to Jewish "priestesses' or rabbis. It has only been in recent times that the breakaway branches of Reform, Conservative, Reconstructionism and Jewish Renewal, have begun recognizing and ordaining female rabbis, and placing them as equals to male rabbis on the pulpit and in the congregation. But there certainly have been key female figures within the tradition, such as Miriam, Deborah, Esther and Ruth, for example.

Miriam was considered a prophet in her own right, as was Deborah. There were three siblings in Moses' family. Moses was the youngest, Aaron was his older brother, and Miriam was the oldest. She played a key role in the story of Moses and the Exodus. She is particularly associated with nurturance and water. During the period of the Exodus and the wandering in the wilderness, in addition to the manna appearing, there was also a mysterious miraculous source of water. Somehow there was a spring that moved with the Hebrews as they wandered in the wilderness after leaving Egypt. The spring moved with them or appeared wherever they went. When Miriam passed away, the spring dried up. She was somehow the force connected with this spring. When her energy left, the spring left. Fortunately, they were about to enter the Holy Land, but they no longer had "the waters of Miriam" as a source for water.

Literal/Fundamentalist vs. Figurative/Symbolic

That brings up the next issue concerning literal/fundamentalist and figurative/symbolic. Literal acts carry figurative meanings. Someone drinking a glass of water can be seen literally as someone just drinking a glass of water, but this simple act contains layers of profound meaning. Someone exists in all the profundity of life, and that someone is receiving essential nurturance, the water of life. It is a profound, deep act, this act of drinking a glass of water. And yet it is ordinary and mundane at the same time. But at all times, it resonates internally as we integrate the profound meaning contained within the simple gesture, sometimes consciously, and always unconsciously. But there is always an impact on some level.

The Red Sea parts, miraculously removing a barrier for the emergence of certain people from their captivity in a narrow land that was choking them. Then it closes against those not ready to emerge, those trying to hold back the new, trying to prevent the emergence. The flesh of the sacrificed animals is permitted as food, but not the blood, for the blood contains the animal life force, the animal nature, and must be forbidden. Do not take a blade to your skin; do not compromise the life force within.

Jealousy and Idolatry

The One God is a jealous God; those who attune to this Oneness must not allow for a second, a separation. There is room for aspects, functions, attributes of this Oneness, but not for separation. Unity must be maintained amidst all apparent diversity. If Unity is lost, all is lost to the separation of idolatry, and thus the gravity of this sin. Idolatry/separation is spiritual death, for the fountainhead of Oneness, of Ultimate Meaning, has been lost. Idolatry must not be tolerated in any form. All actions must be taken within the context of the One. Toward the One, Toward the One…The blessings of the Infinite One originating in the Beyond are transmuted down through the worlds, in various degrees and grades, to its manifestation in the material world for the glorification of the One: Baruch Atah Adonoi Elohaynu Melech Ha'Olam…

Homosexuality

Homosexuality and cross-dressing as abominations. What is the meaning, the teaching here? Polarity/duality is a basic mystical conception/experience. Balance/androgyny/union of forces is the goal, the process. Like poles repel, opposite poles attract. Generally speaking, there needs to be space between male and male, between female and female because of this natural law of repulsion (abomination?) and attraction. But the literal can become too rigid in application. There are always exceptions, and sometimes things aren't as they appear. Outer homosexual attraction may not be a real aberration/abomination when the internal energies of the individuals involved are taken into account.

Circumcision

And circumcision. What about this most significant of events in Jewish life even to this day, an event embroiled in a deep-seated emotional joy? The covenant between God and His Chosen People is sealed/marked by the circumcision on the eighth day of life of the foreskin of the male sex organ. On the face of it, from an objective point of view, this seems quite bizarre. Why should this particular process of cutting off the foreskin of the male sexual organ signify the seal of this covenant? And why is the sexual circumcision taken as a literal physical event when the Torah and Tanak also speak of a "circumcision of the heart" that is obviously not meant as a literal physical event (Leviticus 26:41, Deuteronomy 10:16 and 30:6, Jeremiah 9:25 and Ezekiel 44:7)? Rabbi Aryeh Kaplan also has described a circumcision of the tongue:

"The Hebrew word for 'circumcision' is *Milah*. This same word, however, also means 'word'...The "circumcision of the tongue' refers to the ability to utilize the mysteries of the Hebrew language. It also refers to the ability to probe the mysteries of the Torah. In a more general sense, such circumcision denotes a fluency of speech. One who cannot speak properly is said to have 'uncircumcised lips'...When one is given the power of proper speech, his tongue is said to be circumcised. This is both the 'circumcision' and the 'word' of the tongue. ...Prophecy involves a particularly intense focusing of spiritual energy, allowing the prophet to actually speak in God's name. Prophecy was thus the ultimate level of 'circumcision of the tongue'." *Sefer Yetzirah*, pp 35, 36

Just as the circumcisions of the heart and tongue are seen as inner figurative processes whereby, in the case of the heart, the outer membrane/barrier of the lower animal heart is seen as being removed to reveal the purity of the higher divine heart, and in the case of the tongue, speech is seen as becoming purified and inspired, perhaps so should the sexual circumcision be seen, whereby a process/vow is undertaken to transmute the lower sexual energies to the higher divine calling.

"An eye for an eye, a tooth for a tooth" is consistently and insistently interpreted by Jewish commentators as not meant to be literal. Circumcision of the sexual organ is seen as literal, yet circumcision of the heart is obviously not. The practice of Tefillan and mezuzahs are seen as literal physical directives evolved from passages that could easily be seen as figurative and not literal. How are these distinctions made, what is the criteria for the distinctions, who has made them/is making them, and are they subject to re-interpretation?

Torah As a Description of Involution and Prescription for Evolution

Torah can be seen as a blueprint, a map, a description of creation and the involution of consciousness through inner realms until its final expression in the external world. Torah can also be seen as a prescription for the evolution of consciousness. What is the importance of and distinction between inner practices and outer observances? Do outer observances not consciously linked with their inner significance still have constructive effect on an unconscious level? Do inner practices not linked to outer observances have a more limited effect than if they were linked? If inner practice shapes proper "right action" in the external world of everyday activities and interactions, what is the need for outer ritual observances that in and of themselves do not engage in everyday activities and interactions, but rather, by design and intent, are conducted separately from them in liturgical services?

The Kabalistic model of the four worlds of Atziluth, Briah, Yetzirah and Assiah has somehow emerged from a deep study of Torah. A revelation as to this design: first comes involution: the realm between Adam and Noah is the world of Atziluth, transitioning/involving into the world of Briah; the realm between Noah and Abraham is the world of Briah, transitioning/involving into the world of Yetzirah; the realm between Abraham and Moses is the world of Yetzirah, transitioning/involving into the world of Assiah; and the realm from Moses to the present is the world of Assiah, containing both the culmination of involution and the beginning of an evolutionary ascent back to Yetzirah. Torah is a description of the process of involution/descent, beginning with the highest and most subtle of all realms, from which creation first emanates, down into the final realm of the world of physicality, hammered out to its lowest, most gross level in the period of captivity in Egypt. The emergence from Egypt signaled the beginning of evolution/ascent, and Torah provides the prescriptions for this process.

Denominational Doctrinal Differences

The debates among the Jewish denominations remain. Is both written and oral Torah a perfect, infallible Divine Revelation/Sacred Scripture, a monumental man-made myth, or something in-between? Are the events historical, metaphorical, or both? My own conclusions at the present time: there is certainly a Divine Hand at work here, but at times, there also appears human intervention. There is obvious myth and metaphor at work, but perhaps real historical figures are integrated into these stories and teachings, assuming legendary/mythic proportions. It does not have to be one or the other, as indicated by the above discussion of literalness vs. figurativeness. The truth of the matter, and what matters the most, is that the study of Torah has the magical ability to immerse one in an inner spiritual transformational process far more profound than a mere intellectual exercise. The description of events contain a surface literal meaning, whether or not historical, and contain deeper layers of meaning, again, whether or not historical. So Judaism spans all of these points of view, and the teachings and stories of the Torah remain significant among subscribers to all of these points of view. The lessons learned, the values, the virtues, the morals, the inner essences and practical guidelines for everyday living are remarkably similar regardless of the point of view and differences in outer observances. Externally, the denominations may appear quite different in their observances and beliefs, but internally, much of the same inspiration is attained, and many of the same conclusions are reached. And thus, the enduring magic of the Torah.

The Old Yielding to the New

One obvious repeating theme in the Torah is of the old yielding to the new. Within the context of a strong cultural tradition favoring the first-born, we find repeated stories breaking this mold and depicting younger siblings bestowed with leadership positions instead of the first-borns. Abraham is the oldest son, but his younger son Isaac proceeds with the lineage over his older brother Ishmael. Again, Jacob ascends as the Patriarch over his older brother Esau (albeit, only by a little time, as they were twins). Rueben loses his first-born privileges to Joseph, and in Joseph's absence, the leadership falls primarily to Judah, not back to Rueben. The youngest son, Benjamin, is favored over all by Jacob, as Joseph had been favored before his disappearance and the birth of Benjamin. Ephraim, the younger son of Joseph, is given the blessing of the first-born by Jacob over his older brother and the real first-born, Manasseh. Moses is Aaron's younger brother, and is selected as the primary leader of the Exodus over his older brother.

Perhaps the most interesting is the story of the birth of Zerach and Perez to Judah. They also were twins, and at the time of birth, Zerach's (Sun) hand and arm emerge first, with the midwives marking it accordingly with a crimson thread. However, his arm withdraws, and Perez (Moon) is actually fully born first. So Zerach was actually marked as the first-born, but loses his birthright to his twin brother. This echoes themes from the one episode in the Torah that I have found the most moving of all. In Exodus, Moses goes up to the mountain for the second time, after having smashed the first tablets due to the Golden Calf incident, ashamed, embarrassed and exasperated for and by his people. He pleads for forgiveness, mercy, and more direction and guidance from God so that such transgressions will not happen again. In this mood, as the ultimate advocate for his people, this most humble of all human beings continues to press God for more and more "concessions" of sorts, for direct involvement in the guidance of the people, culminating in what appears to be the most bold request imaginable: he asks God point blank to show him his "glory". God, in a reciprocal mood of ultimate mercy, responds that no human can see his "face" and live, and arranges for Moses to behold as much as any human can bear: "Behold! There is a place near Me; you may stand on the rock. When My glory passes by, I shall place you in a cleft of the rock: I shall shield you with My hand until I have passed. Then I shall remove My hand and you will see My back, but My face may not be seen." The moon is much easier on the eyes than the sun. Perez, the moon, will suffice (El Shaddai), for Zerach, the sun, is too much to bear. The sun, the source of light, makes a brief appearance first to initiate the light, but then the moon comes forward to reflect it in a digestible manner.

The Chosen People and The Promised Land

The traditional orthodox seem to maintain two primary versions to the origins of the concept of "The Chosen People". The first is taken directly from the main text of the Torah. All of mankind failed to take on the responsibilities of the covenant offered by God, as evidenced by the events that led to the expulsion from the Garden of Eden, the Great Flood during the time of Noah, and the Tower of Babel incident during the time of Abraham. God therefore narrowed the offer down to Abraham and his selected lineal descendants through to Jacob and his twelve sons and their descendants. There is a conception here that God "chose" the Hebrew people and there is no explanation as to why, for their history is replete with stories of transgressions comparable to the transgressions of the rejected nations. And yet in their case, God always forgave them and gave them another chance, constantly stating that He would never totally abandon them (although He certainly got close a couple of times!). The second version of "The Chosen People", derived from various sources, is that God offered this covenant to all of the other peoples of the world, and only after they all rejected it, was the offer made to the Jewish people, who accepted it in faith without question, not even knowing what was involved or required of them. These two versions are not contradictory, as they involve a covenant, and by definition, a covenant involves two parties entering into an agreement. There has been a general feeling, however, under the first version, that when God makes an offer, you don't reject it, so there was not really a choice made by the people, but rather that God made the choice, and that was the end of it. (This parallels a common sentiment among my household members growing up that "you can't say no to the Rabbi" – whenever our Rabbi asked something of us, we did it. Of course, the Rabbi never asked us to do anything we were not capable of doing, but perhaps sometimes things that we wouldn't have volunteered to do if not asked). The second version introduces the idea of the inferiority of all of the other peoples of the world having rejected the offer, and that the Jewish people had the option to accept or reject, and chose to accept, so it was ultimately their choice, and they are entitled to enjoy all of the benefits and privileges of this choice, especially since it was rejected by everyone else.

Under either of these conceptions, the terms and nature of the covenant are the same: in exchange for complying with the 613 commandments, God will grant the Jewish people special status among all the peoples of the world as the spiritual leaders for all of humankind, and along with this status, the Promised Land is granted to them, identified by various boundaries in the general area we refer to as Palestine/The Middle East.

The basis of their claim to the land and state of Israel is grounded by the Orthodox in this biblical covenant: God granted us this land, God has allowed others to occupy this land from time to time, but the Jews' right and claim to ultimate ownership of this land is grounded in the Bible. The Orthodox likewise point to biblical sources to justify their view that the Jewish people are this exclusive club charged with carrying on their special role of being the spiritual leaders of all mankind, and the sooner all of the other nations recognize this role, the better off will all of humanity be. The Jewish people are not only serving themselves, they are serving all of humankind. While there are fundamentalist fanatics in branches of Eastern religions, it appears that the Eastern traditions are generally more tolerant of a view that there are many paths to the Divine, and that no one path is necessarily superior to another. It seems more prevalent in Western traditions to find fundamentalist doctrines that theirs is the only way, with accompanying zealous missionary movements designed to try to convert everyone else in the world to their way, and anyone who does not convert is condemned to eternal damnation. The orthodox Jewish belief recognizes that there are other ways and other paths, but they are all subservient and inferior to the Jewish way, which is the superior way, and needs to be recognized as such. Conversion to this superior path is possible and has always occurred, but should be actively discouraged. Interpretations of the Torah and its commentaries are replete with building and reinforcing this concept of the superiority of the Jewish people over all others (witness, for example, the Stone commentaries about the descendants of Ishmael and Esau; or, as a contemporary example, the popular Jewish joke with the punchline that while the Pope can call God for $1.00, a Rabbi can call God for 25 cents, because for the Rabbi, it is a local call). Given this view and attitude, it is no wonder why Jews have been persecuted over the millennium out of sheer resentment.

Islam and Christianity, both emerging out of Judaism, extend the superiority concept a step further. Instead of claiming an exclusive club and placing high barriers around membership as Judaism does, fundamentalists of both of these religions proclaim theirs is the only truth and only way, and undertake to convert everyone to their way, upon penalty of eternal damnation. Add to this the Christian belief that the Jews were responsible for Christ's crucifixion, and the Muslim/Arab resentment of the Jews with its roots going all the way back to the prevalent Jewish interpretation of the story of Ishmael, placing him in a derogatory light, and it is no wonder that there is such significant cultural, ethnic and religious strife in the world.

What has become clear to me in my study of Torah is that it is a text encompassing a teaching meant for a specific segment of humanity known and identified as Jews. It appears that some of it is of Divine Origin, some may have historical references and bases, some is obviously metaphor, and some has been tinkered with by people with certain agendas. There are clear indications, especially in Genesis, that there are to be other sacred teachings and texts for other peoples and nations who are no less inferior or superior or spiritual. The Torah and all it has generated is one piece in a patchwork quilt of a vast range of spiritual/religious teachings generated for the benefit of humankind. The New Testament is another piece, as is the Koran, the Vedas, the texts of Buddhism and Taoism, and other spiritual texts and scriptures.

There is a provincial tendency among various groups, be they religions, cultures, nationalities, ethnic groups, schools, fraternities, clubs, etc., to think that they are the best. Many such groups have their own particular stories, legends and myths to support their view of their uniqueness and special status. You can see this in national pride, religious pride, school pride, etc. There is probably an isolated group of Eskimos living somewhere in the remote regions of the Arctic Circle whose members genuinely believe that they are the center of the universe, the guardians of the real Truth, and are to play a central role in the spiritual awakening of all mankind. You can probably find similar beliefs among almost every such discrete group anywhere in the world. It is one thing to think we are unique, because every single individual is unique, and there are defined groups who share certain qualities and perhaps certain missions and functions in the greater tapestry of life. It may even be okay to think we are all special, because, again, each individual and group, as part of their uniqueness, has something special to contribute. The danger, the conflicts, the wars, arise when we start thinking we are superior, we are the center of the universe, the axis upon which the world spins, we are the leaders whom others should follow, we have the right to claim dominion over other peoples or lands or both. Then we point to our particular sacred texts and twist, contort and distort them to justify these positions and actions.

Fortunately among Jewish movements and thought, there are those who do not subscribe to a doctrine of superiority. There is a growing world view among Reform, Reconstructionist, and Jewish Renewal circles that Jews are a piece of this patchwork quilt of life. Each piece is unique in its own way and serves to maintain the whole in its own special way. Only through such a viewpoint shared by all of the peoples and religions of the world can there dawn even the faint promise of any type of lasting world peace and harmony. This is the basis for real acceptance and acknowledgement of the validity of the diversity that obviously exists in the world. Such acceptance and acknowledgement amounts to more than mere tolerance. Although true tolerance may be a positive and necessary step in the right direction, the word "tolerance" carries with it a somewhat negative connotation of "bearing with" or "reluctantly putting up with" something, even if it is not much liked or accepted. At some point, we need to move beyond merely tolerating diversity to honoring, embracing and celebrating it. For God, the Conductor, did not mean for the orchestra to contain only one instrument. For Heaven's Sake, let's come to our senses and allow all of the instruments to play in harmony and not in discord. Amen.

ABOUT THE AUTHOR

Steven J. Gold, BA Antioch College, Philosophy and Religion; JD Emory Law School, is the founder/director of the Yoga and Judaism Center in Atlanta, GA. He has been a student, practitioner and teacher of spiritual self-realization and its related philosophy and psychology for many years. Over the past thirty years, he has read or studied with many eastern and western teachers of spirituality and "New Age" thought and practice. He is an initiate and practitioner in the Tradition of the Himalayan Masters, as propagated in the West by the late Sri Swami Rama of the Himalayas. This broad-based tradition includes the classical Ashtanga Yoga/Raja Yoga and meditation systems of Patanjali and the Advaita Vedanta systems and philosophy of Shankara. He is a graduate of the Karin Kabalah Center course on *Kabalah: A Process of Awakening,* and has continued a course of self-study of Torah and mystical Judaism in light of yoga for more than 5 years. He has studied with Rabbi Joseph Gelberman, Rabbi Gedalia Fleer, Rabbi Eliyahu Schusterman, Rabbi Arthur Waskow, Rabbi Phyliss Berman, and Zev ben Shimon Halevi.

The mission of The Yoga and Judaism Center is to provide an avenue for the awakening, nurturance and expression of spirituality with a focus, although not exclusively, on the mystical traditions of Yoga/Vedanta and Judaism/Kabala. We seek the common threads that exist between these and various other spiritual and mystical traditions, exploring the possibilities for a new synthesis relevant to the spiritual needs of today. Yogis and non-yogis, Jews and non-Jews, are all welcome.

To contact the author, for more information about the Yoga and Judaism Center, or to order a book: PO Box 1769, Decatur, GA 30031; yajcenter@aol.com; http://stores.lulu.com/yajc; www.lulu.com; http://yajcenter.blogspot.com [blog]; 404-377-1161, fax 404-377-4124.